3		5		6	9	4		
6	9	4	7	2		3	5	1
1	7		3	4	5	2	9	6
	8		9					5
				8			4	
		3	5	1	2	9		8
5	6	7	4			8		9
	1	2			6		7	
8	3	9				6	1	4

						[illegible]	[illegible]	[illegible]
5	[illegible]	[illegible]	[illegible]	[illegible]	[illegible]	[illegible]	[illegible]	[illegible]
7	[illegible]	[illegible]	[illegible]	[illegible]	[illegible]	[illegible]	[illegible]	[illegible]
	2	[illegible]	[illegible]	[illegible]	[illegible]	[illegible]	[illegible]	[illegible]
			[illegible]	[illegible]	[illegible]	2		
9		[illegible]	[illegible]	6	2	3	4	
2	1		4				6	
3	6	5	9		1	4		7
	7			2	6	1	8	

6	8	9				5		4
	1	7		6	9		3	
	3	2		8	5		9	6
	5		8	1	6	3		
1	7			4	2			5
		8		5	7	4		
8	4		2			6	5	9
7	6			9		2	4	3
2	9	5				1	7	8

8	2			5	6		4	1
		6	7		8			
1					4	8		
6	8		9		3			4
2	9		8	4		6	3	
3			5	6		1	8	9
4	6	3		8	5	9	7	2
				2	7	3		5
7	5	2		3	9		1	

7		5		2		4	6	9
				4	5			
	4		1			8		
9	6	7	8	1	4			5
8		1		5			4	6
						7	1	
1	9	3	7		2	5	8	
		8			1	6	9	7
6	7		5					3

7		2	1		3	9		
8	1			7	9	2		4
		9	8		5		3	
	6	4		8	7	5	1	3
	3		4	1	2	6	9	7
		7			6	4		8
		1	3	5	4	8	6	
3		6	7	9				
4	8		2		1			

5		4			2	8	7	1
			8			5	6	2
	2	8			6	4	3	9
						1	2	5
						3	8	
		5	7	8	3		9	
	5			9		2		
6	9	1	2				4	
7	8		3		4		5	6

	5	2	6	8		4	9	7
9		6	7		5	3	8	
		8	2	9			1	
	7		9	4	2	8	6	5
2	6		5	3			7	
		5		6	7	2	3	
	1	3	4			7		
	8	7		2	6	9		
5	2							3

		1		9	7	5		2
2	4	5		1		9		7
	7	9	2	6		4	3	1
						2		8
						6	1	9
9				7	1	3		5
1	6	4	7	2	9	8		3
	9	8	6		3	1		4
	5	2		8	4	7	9	

9	6			3	4	2	8	
1			8	2		6		
	2				7	3	4	
6	8		4	9	3	7	1	
		3		7			6	8
7			6	8		4	5	
8	7	6	2	1	9			
4		2	3	5			7	
3	5	1	7	4	6			9

		5		8	4	1	7	6
			5		2			9
9	4						3	5
	1	3	4	5			6	2
		4	1	2		3		8
		2	3			7		
3	2		8					7
6	5	9	7		3			
4	8			9	5			

4	9	2		7			1	8
	3		2	1	5		4	9
					4	2	3	
6				4		1		
	5	4		6	2		8	3
9	2	8		3	1	4	6	7
3	8	9	4	5			2	
5	6		1				9	
	4	1		9	8		7	5

1			8		9	4	3	
8	3	4	2			6		9
9	2	5	6	4		1		
2	4		3	7	6			
6							2	
		9	1	8	2			
5		1	9	2	8		4	7
	8	2	7	3	1	5		
	9	3	5	6	4		8	1

6	8					1	7	
1				4				2
7		9		1				3
4	3	5	6			9	2	1
9	1			3		8	5	7
8			1	5		3		6
3	6	4	9	2		7		8
2	9			6	1	4		
5	7	1	3		4			9

1		6		4	5	2	3	9
3	4	7					5	1
9		5	1				4	
	3		5	7			9	
7	6		4		9		8	
4	5			8		1	7	2
	7	4	2			9	1	8
2	1				4	3		7
6	9		8			4	2	5

	1	7	6	4	8		2	
2				3	5		4	
3				7		5	1	6
7		8	4	6		3		
6	3			2	7	1		
			8	5		6		2
	5	6					3	1
	9	2	3		6			8
1	7		5	8	4	2	6	9

		2	3		9		7	8
9				5	6		3	4
	6		7	8		9		
1			8	2	5		9	6
2		7		6	4	8	5	3
6	8			7	3	4		2
8		6			7		4	1
4		9	6	1	2			
	2				8			

	9	7		3				
	8		7	6	5	9	3	
6			2			8	7	5
1			3			5	4	
4		2				3		1
	5			4	2	6	8	7
9	1			2	7	4	5	
	2							9
7		5	9		1			

6			8			2	3	
4	5			3	2		7	
	2	8	5	7			9	
1							8	7
5	7	6	1		9			2
9	8	3		4		5		
2						7	1	
7		1	9		3		5	
	3	4	7		5			

	2			6	4		8	
4	7	9		1		3	5	
5	8		9	3		1	4	2
	9	4					7	
		1	8		5	9	2	4
				9			1	3
6	3	5	7	8	2		9	
7	1	2	3		9	5	6	
		8		5				

5			9	6	3	1	8	
3			8	1	2			7
1	8	2	4	7		9	6	
	6					7		8
	3		7	5				4
	7				9	2	3	1
	1		5	9		8	2	6
	2	4		8		3		5
			2		7	4		

	4	1	6				8	
7	2	8	9	3		4	5	6
				2				
3	8	4	2		6		9	
	7			8		2	6	1
2	1			9	5	8	4	
4	9		1	6		5	2	
		2				6		
1	6		8	7	2	9	3	

			6	3		9		5
9				4	8		1	2
	3	5			9	8	4	6
6	9	1			2	7	8	4
4			8		6	5	3	
5	8	3		7				
				6		4	5	
7	2			8		1		3
3	5	6	4	1		2	9	

5		2	7	6	3	9		
				2	9	7	5	3
9	3		5	4			1	
8						3		9
3			8	5	2	1		7
6		1			4	5		
1		9		8		2	7	
2	5		4				9	1
7		6		9	1		3	

	6		5	4			9	1
2			6	9	1	3		
9					8		5	6
6	3			5		7		8
4	1					5	3	
5		2	8					
8		7	9		6			3
	2		4	8		9		
3			7		5	6	8	

7		8		6			9	5
9	1		4		5			2
	3	5				6	8	4
5					6			
	6		7	5	9		4	3
4				1	3	5	6	
		2	6	7	4	8		
6	8	4	5	3	1	9		
1		7	9		8	4	3	6

			6	9	7	3		4
		5		3			9	2
	9				5	6		
1					2	5	4	
		8						
5	6	4		1	3	8		7
		3		8	1		6	
2		6				4	1	3
9	5	1	3		6		7	8

3	7			4	5		9	
		5	7	9	8	1	6	
		9		3	2		7	
6	1	8		2	7		5	9
	4	3	9		6	8		
		7		1	4			
9			2		3	7	8	
	3	6		8		9		
	8		4	7	9			5

	9		3		2	8		6
	6	3	5	8				4
4						5	3	7
7		1			8	6	4	5
2		5	7		6		8	1
6	8			1		7	2	3
9			1	6		3		8
		4			9	1		
8		6		7			5	

4	9		2		5	7		
2					1		5	4
	5	1		4				
1	4	6	3	7	8	5	2	9
	3			9	2		6	1
				1	6	8		
	6		1	5			3	7
		2	6			1		
	1	9				6	4	5

7	2	4	9				6	3
	6	3			4			9
1				3	5	7		
	5	2		6	8	1	9	7
8	1				7	3		
3						2	4	8
9	4	7	5	1	3	6	8	
2			7	4	6	9		1
6		1	8		2		7	5

1					2	5	7	
3		4	5		7			2
7	5	2	8	4	9	1	6	3
	2		4	8			5	9
		9	7				2	1
8	1		2		3		4	6
2	7		6	3	8		9	
		6	1	7	5		3	8
	8		9	2				7

		9	4	5		7		1
4				7	3	6		2
3			2				4	
7			8		2		9	6
8		2	5	9	6	4		3
		6		4	7		2	8
9			1	8				7
2	6		7		5		1	4
	7				9		8	5

3	9				7			8
8	7	2		3		6	1	
1	5	6	2		8	7		3
9	6		3	8		5		
	4	8	7	5	1		3	6
		3		9			7	
	8		6	1	4		2	
6			5		9		8	7
	2	9	8	7	3	1		5

4		5	6			9		
2		7	5	9				
8	9	1	3		2			6
	7	4	8		6	2		
	2	3	1	4	9	6	7	8
6	8			2	5			4
7			4					9
3						7	6	2
9	5	6		8		3		

	3	7	5	2	4		6	9
6	2		3				8	4
		1	6	9	8		7	2
			9	5	2	7	1	8
1			8	7	6		3	
					3			
	1	4	7		5	8	2	3
7		5		3			4	
2			4	8	1	9	5	7

6		5		7	4	2	3	
	1	7		2		5	8	
		2	5		1		9	
			2	3	7	1	6	4
2	7	4	1	8	6			3
	6		4		9	8		
	2				8			
	4	1	7	9		6	2	8
	8					7	4	9

3	1	5		7	6	9		8
	9		1	8				6
8	6	7		3	2		1	
6	5		2		9	3	8	7
4		2			3	6	5	9
		9		6	8			2
5	7	6	3	2		8		
			8		7	2	6	5
	2	8				4		

3			2	9		1	8	
4	2		5	1	8	3		6
8	6				7	5		
	1	4	7		9	8	6	
7	9	2			3			1
		3	4		1			2
		8			2			
	7		1	6	4		3	
		6	8	3	5	9	1	

4	6	8	1	5	9		2	
7				3	6		1	
3		5		2	8	4		9
	3	6	5	7	4		9	
				8	1			
5		2	9	6	3	1	4	
	9	3	6	1	2			
2	7		3	9			8	1
	5	1	8	4				2

1		5	7			8		
2	8			1	4	9	7	
	3	7		9		6	1	
7	1	8	2					
		2	9	6	8	7	3	
9		3	1					
3	5	9				1	6	
	7				1			9
	2		3	5				7

3	2		6	7		4	8	
9			1		4			7
				3		9		
	7	3	8				9	4
	1		4	2		8		6
	4		7	9	1	3		2
7		6	9	1				8
		4	3	6				
8			5	4	7	6	1	3

	5	9	7	4		8		6
	2			3		4	9	
7	6		8	9		2	5	
6	9	3	1	7	4		2	
	7	1					6	9
5	8		9	6	3			
2	3	6		1	7			4
		7	4			6	3	5
9	4		3	8		1		2

	1	4				7		
3						4	9	2
2	7	6				8	1	3
			4	2				1
4	2	9	7				3	5
1		8	5		9			7
8			6	5	1			
	5		8		4	1		9
7			3			5	6	8

5			4	3			9	7
7		9	5			4	1	3
	1					6		5
9	3	8	6	7				
6		1		5	2	9	8	
			9		8	7	3	
		6	2	9		3		1
2	9						6	8
			8		5		7	

8				4		2		5
		9			5		8	7
2	1			6	7		9	
	8		7		9	4	2	6
6	9		3	2	1			
7	5							9
9	7	1	4	3	6		5	2
		8	1				6	
	2			9	8	7	4	1

6					2	9	5	8
		2	6	5				4
9				3	8		6	1
	5	6	9		7	1		2
	9				4	5	8	6
4	8	1		6	5	7	3	9
5	6			2	1			7
	4		7	9	3			5
		9	5	4	6		1	

			9	2	8			4
	3	2				8		
	8		1				6	
2		8	5			9		6
5	1		6	8	4		7	3
3	7	6		1	9	5	4	
6	5	3				1	8	7
7			8	5	1	6	3	9
8	9			7			2	5

3		1		7	5	2	4	
8		2		3	1			5
5	4	7	2			1	3	6
		9	1	8	7			4
7	3		5				1	
	5	4	3		2			7
				5				
	8	3		2		5		
		5	8		3	4		9

8				1	7		5	
5	4					6	9	7
3	6				5			2
		8	3			7		
1	3			7	4	9	8	
2	7		5	8		3	6	
6					2		7	
7		5		3		2	4	6
4	2	9				1		8

2	3		7		1	9		8
1	8	6	9			4	7	
7	4		3					5
9		8	4	7	3	6	5	1
3		7		8	6	2		
		4	1			3		7
4		2		1	7		3	
6		3	2	9		8	1	4
					4			2

					4		1	9
	6		8			5	4	2
				9		6	3	7
9	8		6		1	2		
		3	4	2		9	6	
6		1	3				8	
		7	5	1	6			4
	5	2	7			1	9	6
	1					7		8

	9	1	8			2	6	7
3				9	7	5	4	
4	7	6		2				8
	1	3	9		6			
9		8	5		2	6		
7	6			1	3			
		4	7	5	8	9		6
	5			4	9		8	
				6	1		5	

8	2			6	5		3	1
4		3			7			8
6	1	5		3	8			7
3	5	1					7	
7	8		5		6	3		
	6				3			4
9	7	2		5	1	6		
		6	3	7	2	1	8	9
1	3	8	6	4			2	5

7			9	1	6			
	5	6		2				9
2		9	8		7	6	1	
8		1	5		2	9	3	
5	7		6	9	3		4	
		4	7		1	5	2	
4	2	8	1	7	9		6	
			2			4	7	
3		7		6		8	9	

8	1		9		2	5	3	7
	9	2	3			8	1	
					8			
2		8		7		1	6	
6	7	5	8		1	9	2	4
	4	1	5			3	7	
4	2	9	1	8	7			3
3			6	9	4		8	1
		6	2	5		7		9

	2	7			1	5		
	9	3	6		5	2		
5		6	7	3				
7		8		2	4	9		
	3	4			6	7	5	2
1	6		5	7		3	4	
6	4		1		3			7
2		5	9	6	7	1		
3		1	2	4				

2			7	9			5	1
9	5			3		2	7	
		8				3	6	9
	4	7	8		2	9		3
			9	6				2
5	9	2	4					
4	2		1		9	7		6
	6	1	2	7				
7	8		3					

6		1	8	9	2		3	4
	7		6		1		5	9
9		4		3				6
5				1	6		7	2
2	6							1
1			2	7	4		8	
			7	6		9	1	3
			1			5		
7	1		4	5	9	2	6	

	5	1	4				9	6
9				5			2	4
4					1	3	8	5
5								
7	6	3	9	4		8		
	1	9	6	8			5	
6			8	1		2	4	3
1	3		2	6	9			
	7	2	5	3	4			1

	3	2	1		8	7		
	1	7	5		2	8	4	9
				6	7		2	
2		6					5	
3			9		6		1	
8	7	1	2	5	3		9	6
7	2					5	8	1
	4		7			6		2
5	6	8	3		1			4

			9	7				4
9	8	2	4				7	5
	3	7		1	5			6
			5	2		9	3	
5	1		7					2
		3	1		6		5	7
3	7		8		1		4	
			6		7	5		3
1	4	5			2			8

4	2	1	6	9			3	
5		6	7		4	9	8	1
	7	8				6		2
2	9	5		1				
3			2	8		5		6
8	6		9		5			4
6					1	2		
7	5			6	9	4	1	
1		9	5				6	

4	3		8		1			7
		2	9			3	1	
		7			5	6	9	
7	6	3	5		9			
1		5	4	7	8	9		
		8			6	7	2	5
	7	1	6	8		5	4	9
5			7					3
3	9				4	8	7	

		9		2		4	3	6
6	7	4	3		8			
3	5				4	1		8
1		7	9	6				
			4	5		7	9	1
	9		8	7	1		4	2
4	3		1		9		5	
9					5	8		4
7	8	5	2	4		3	1	

		2	8		1			4
1		7					8	2
	8				5			3
7	9	4	1			2		
2	6	3	7	5	8			
	1		9	4	2			6
	3	9		1	4			7
	7	1	2				4	
4	2	8	3			6	1	

	1		2	7	9			
4		8	3			7		2
3	2	7	4	6		5		1
		2	7	4	6	3		9
9		4			1	8	7	6
1	7					2	5	4
			1		2		4	7
			8		7	6	3	5
7			6	3		1		8

		9		6			1	
	1			9	7			
2			8		4	9	3	
					9		2	5
9				5	3	6	8	
5	8	6	2	7	1			4
4	9	3	7	2				
8	5	1		4	6			3
7	6				8	5		9

4			2	9		6	7	1
5		9	6			2		
2				1	3	4		
6				8	7	3		4
	4	1			6	9		
	5	3		4	2	1	6	
3		4			8			
	2	7	5	6		8	4	
9	8		4	3	1	7	2	6

8				1		3	9	4
			5	3		1	6	
		6		8				
7	6		8	4	3	9	2	5
5	2		7	6		4		
	4		1	5		6	7	
4	1		6		5		3	9
	8		3		1	5		7
3	5	9	4		8	2		6

	6					8	3	9
		2			8	4	7	1
		4	7	1			5	6
	8	5			1	3	9	4
			3	6	5			
	3	1	4				6	5
4					6	5		8
	1	6	8					7
9			1		7			3

4		2	1	3		5	7	9
	1	9		2	8	3		4
	6							1
		3		7		4		
6	4		9		2	7	3	8
2			3		4			5
1								3
5				1		8		2
		4	2			6	1	7

3	8	9		5	1	4	7	
2	6	5				3	9	
	7			2	9	8		
	2	7	1		6	9	3	4
	1			3			2	
			4			1	5	
	5	8		6	3	2		
7	9		2	4		5	1	6
	4	2	9					3

5	6		9		4		2	3
3	9		6	7			5	1
	1			5				9
1	3	5		4			8	6
					6	5		
6	8	4	1		5	2		7
8	7	3		6			4	
9	4	1	7	2				
2				3	1		9	8

8		7	4	6				
4							5	6
2	6		7				8	4
9	1	8	2	3	6	5	4	
	2		5	9				1
3			1	7			2	9
5	7	3	6	4	9			
1		4	3	2	7		6	5
6	9	2		5	1			3

9		8	1	6	2			5
5	3		8		7	2	6	
				3	5	7	9	
8	9	5		2		6		3
7	6	2		8	1		5	
	1		9	5				7
	4	9		7		1		6
3		6		1	9		7	4
	5				3			2

3				9		6	4	
	2			8	6	3		5
7				4			9	8
	9		6	5	4		3	7
	5	7		3	1	4	6	
	6		2	7	8		1	9
6		9	8	2	7			4
5		2	3		9		8	6
	7				5	9		3

1	3			4	6		7	9
6		7	1		8	3		4
9		5		3	2	1	8	
4		2	9	6		8	3	7
	9	6	3				2	1
7	8						9	5
		9	2		4	5		8
			8		9		1	3
8	5		6	7		9	4	

	3	2	7		6		9	
9	5	4		3			6	
6	7	8			9			2
	4	9			7	1		
2			3	6	4	5	8	
	6	3	1	9		7		
7	2	6	5	1			4	3
4			6	7	3	2		8
			9		2			1

4	7						5	8
		6		7	8	2		
5					6		1	
2	6	7			3	8		
				8	7	9	6	3
		8		4	5		7	2
			9		4	7	2	6
			7			4	8	9
	9		8		2	5		1

4	2	5		3	9			
		8		4	1	5		
3		1	6				4	9
7	4					8	9	
5						4	3	7
8	1				3			5
9	5		1	2				6
1		4				7	5	2
2			3	5	7	9	1	4

	1		6	4			2	8
		8	5	2	7	4		
6	2	4			9	3		
5		2	3	8	6		9	
1	7	9	2	5	4	8	6	3
3					1	2		4
	5	3			2	7		
4		1		7	8	5		2
		7	4					1

	1	4			5		9	
	6	5	7	4			2	3
2	9	7					5	4
9			5	7	4		8	1
		8		3		2	7	
	7			8	6	3	4	9
7	3	9		6		5	1	
			1			9	3	2
1		2						7

5	9	2	3	1		4		
3	1	4	5	7		2	8	9
			4		9		3	1
7			6	5		9		3
9	3				4	6		5
			1			8		
	7					1	9	8
		5		4			6	
	2				1			4

				5		8		
6	9		3		8	4	7	5
1	5	8	7		4		3	
	6	7			3		2	
8			9			3		6
3	1	9		2		7	5	
				8	9	1		
4	3		5					
9			2	3		5	4	

		9			8	7	3	
					4	5	2	1
3		4					9	8
	9		8	5		2		6
2							7	3
1		6	2	7			5	9
	3		7	1	2	9	6	
9		2	4			3		
	7	1	9	3		4	8	2

2	8	3		9	4	5	6	
			2	3	8	4	9	7
				6				8
	7		9		5	6	3	
	5	2			7			4
8			3				1	
4			1		9	2	7	6
7				2	6	8	5	
5						1		9

6	2					5		9
		7	4	6	5			1
			9		7		4	
1	9	3	6	8		7	5	
8	7	5	2	9		3		4
4	6	2		5		1	9	
	8	6	1	7			3	5
	5		8	4			2	7
7	4	9				8	1	6

1	6		4	3	7			8
4	7	2	1		9	5		
	9	3		5		7		1
5	1		3	6	2			9
3	2			9		6		7
9			7					2
7	5	8	9	2		1	3	
6		1		7	3		9	5
2					5		7	

1	9					3	6	2
4	2		1		3			9
	3	6	2	9				
2	8	3	9					
9	7				6	5	1	3
5	6			7	4	2		
6	1		4	3	2		8	5
3		8	7	1	5			6
7	5			8		1		

			6	1	2		9	4
4		9	8	7	5	6	3	1
6	7	1	4	3	9	2		5
		3				1	7	8
		4		2			6	9
1	6	7			8		5	
9	4		1	6	7		2	
7				8	4	5		
8					3	9		

3		2	9	6		8		5
6	9	8	4	5	3	2	7	
4	5	1		8	7	6		
1	6	9	7		8			4
8	2				5			9
			6			1	8	
	8	7		4	9		3	6
9								
5	4				2			

6	7	8		5	1	2		4
			6	4		8		
9			2					
5	6		3	7		9	2	1
7			1	2				8
1			5	6	9		4	
	1		4		2	5		
			7		5			
4	2	5		9		3	1	

	7		3	8	6		9	
8	1		9				7	
	9	4		5	7	8	6	
	2		6	3	1	4		7
4	8	1	7	9	5		2	
		7		4	2	5	1	
	6		4	7			5	
7	4			6		9	3	1
9	5				3	7	4	6

		6	3	1				5
4				5	9	6	3	
3			4				7	
2	3		9		5			
	9			2		7		
6	4	5		8	7			3
9	2		5			3		
		3	2		4		8	
5		4	8	3	1	2		9

		7	4	9			5	
2	6	9	3	8	5		1	4
5			1		7			
8	4	5	9	1	2			7
7	2		8	5		4		1
9		3			4	2		5
			6	7			2	3
6		8	2	3	1			9
	9	2	5	4				6

4		6		2	1	9		
	1			7		5		6
	7	8	9	3		2	1	4
	9	3	1		5		2	
	2		7	6	3			5
	6	5	2	8	9		7	3
	8	9					6	1
	5	7	3				4	
3	4		6	9			5	

3		8		6	7		2	4
		1	9	5		6	3	7
7	5		3		2	1		
1	6	3	5		4	9	7	2
	2		6					
8	7	4	2	1	9	3		
			4			7	9	3
	3		7		6		5	
	1		8			2		6

			7	3	6	1	9	4
7						3	6	
			8	4				2
		1		8	3	5	4	7
	4	8		6	7	9	1	3
9	7		5	1	4	8		6
	3	5	4					
	8		6					5
	2	7	3	5				9

8	9	3				5	1	2
5				1	9	8	3	6
1		6		5		9		7
3		8	4	9	2	6		1
7			3		1			5
		2			7			
2	4		1	3			9	8
		7	9	2		1	5	4
9	8	1			5		6	3

	5	4				8		
	7	9	4	3	8	2	5	
	3		5		9		4	1
9				6	4		3	5
	6	3		1				
		5		9			2	
6	2	8			7	9	1	
5	9	7		4	2			8
	4					5		

5		2					7	
8						2	4	6
9		7	6	2	3	5	1	8
6			8	1	2		5	
	7	9	3	6		8	2	
2	5	8	9	7	4			
	2	6	4	8	7	1	9	5
4	8	5				7	6	
7		1	5	3				

2		4	6	9	7	5		
9	1				5	6		
5	6				3	4		2
1	8	9	7	5	2		6	4
6			9	3	4		1	
7			8			2	5	
					8	9		3
	9	6	2	7		8	4	5
	5		3				7	6

1	8	9		7			6	
6				8	3	1		
3			6	9	1	4		5
8	5			6	4		9	3
		3	5				4	8
				3	9	5		
5			3	4	6	2		7
	3				8			4
		1	9				3	

2			3	7		6	9	
7	1	5				3	8	
6			8	1	4	2	5	
	2		6			4	1	5
8				4	1		3	
4	5		2			8	7	6
		4			2	5		
			7		9			
	3		4	5			2	9

7	9	8			5	6	3	2
4	2	1	7	3		8	9	
			9		2	7	1	4
1				6				
	7		4			5		9
	4	6		9	3		7	
	1			7	8		5	
9				5				1
5	6	2	3	1		4		7

5		6			9	7	4	3
2	4	9	5			6		
8	7	3		4			9	5
3	8		9				5	2
			7	5	4	1		8
4	5			2		9	6	7
	3		8			5	1	
1		8					7	9
	6		1	9	3	8	2	

				3		2		
8	3	4	2	6	5	1	9	7
5	6	2	7			4		3
6			8	1				
3		1	6	2	4	8		
4	2	8	3	5	9	7		
	4	3	5			9	7	
	1	5				6	2	8
9	8		1		2	5		4

	4		5					
9	5	6			7	8	1	
1	2		6				5	
7		5		6			3	4
6	9	2		3	5	1	7	8
		1				5		6
		9		5	1	7		
2		4						5
	7	8	3	2		9		1

6			1		2			
	2					8		6
4	3			7	8	9	2	
5		8	2			6		7
1	4	2		6	7	5	3	
		7	5			2	8	4
8			9			1		3
9	5		7	8			6	2
	1		4	5				

3	1		7	8			9	4
	7	6	2	1	9	3	8	
	2		4	3	5	7	1	6
2					8			9
		8	9	6		5		1
	6	4			1			
1			8	5	7		6	
				9	3		7	
	8		1	4	2	9		3

				1	9	8		
9		1	5	6		4		3
6		5	3				9	
	5		7	2			1	4
					5	6	3	2
		4					8	5
5	9	2	6	3			4	8
7	6			8	1		2	
4	1			5	2	3		7

8	7		5	6				2
	3	6		8				7
		5	9					1
	9	8	3				2	6
	5		6	2		4	7	8
	6	2	7		8	1	3	9
5			2	9	6			4
6			8		7	2	9	5
9		7	1	4	5	6	8	3

9		5		8			7	6
2	1		4	9		3		5
8	6		7		5			4
6	9	8	5				3	
	7	2	6		4	8	5	9
			8	2				1
		6	1	5	7		2	
5			2	4	8		1	7
7	2					5	4	

1	9			8	5	7		2
	4		6				1	9
7	6	2		3		4		
	1	7					9	
2		4				6	3	
			7	4	8	5	2	
3	7						4	6
	5		1	9				
6	2	1	3	7	4		8	5

			6		3			
3	7	2	9	8		4		6
6				2		3		8
	9	7		5		6		2
5		6	1	3				
2	3		7	9	6	1		
	2			6	5	9	7	1
	6	5	3		9			
8	1		2			5	6	

	8			1	4		7	5
	5			3		4	1	6
1	9		7			2	3	8
	4		6			7		
	6	8	4	7	1			
2		7		5				4
	2	9		4		5		
		5	8				9	3
					7	6	4	2

9	8	6			5			
			9			5		8
7	1	5				4		6
1		9		7		2	8	3
			4	2		9		7
5		2	3	9	8			1
4	6		8		9	1	2	5
	9	1		5	2	3		
2		3		1			7	9

		1	4	8	6		7	2
3		4		7			6	
	8	6	5		3	9		1
6	7	9		4		5	1	3
			9	5		7		
8	1	5		3	7	4		
	9	8		6			5	
4	6			9		1		8
5	3	7	8	1		6	9	4

4	1				5	3		6
3			1					
			7			8	1	4
9	6	8		2	3			7
2	7	4		1				3
			4	8	7	6	9	
7			3	5				1
	5							
8	4	1	6	7		2	3	5

					3		2	9
2						5	1	
1	9	6		2		7	3	8
6	1		9			3		4
		2			1	9	8	7
			3	5		2	6	1
		1			6	8	4	3
	6	8	7	4				2
	2	4		3	8	6	7	5

	2	8	9				5	3
		4	5	3	7			2
7			6	2	8	4		1
5	8	2	4	7		1		6
4			3	1	6	2		
1			8			9	4	7
8			1	9	3		2	4
	6	1						
2				6	5	3		

2	1		7					9
8						2	5	
3	4		2		8	7	1	
	5	1	9	3			2	
7	3			6	2	4		
	9			8	1	5		7
	8	3			4	9		
		7				1		4
1		4	8	7			6	5

3			7	9	5		1	8
4	5	7				6	9	
1	9		3	4	6			
	3	9		7	4		8	
6			9	2		5	4	
	4			6	1	2	3	
	7	4				9		1
8		6	4	5				2
	2					8		4

	5		4			9		7
		7	5	3	8			4
	6	1		7		8	5	3
1			3	9		5		
	3			5	4		9	
	9	5		1	2	4		
	7	9	1		3			5
		3	9			1	7	6
5			7	8		3	4	

1	7		4	6	9	8		3
6	4					2		7
9	5		7	3	2	1		4
7	8	6					3	1
		4	8		5			
5	1	9	3			4		
	3			2	7	9		
	9	1	5	8			4	6
	6	7		4	1	3		5

3	4	1	9	2	6	7	8	5
7	6		4	5		1	2	9
5	9	2	1					
		9				6	3	
			2	1		8		4
4					9			2
2		6	5	3				8
	1	4	7			3		
8		5			4	2		

8			7	9	4			1
3		7	1			6	2	
	5	9		2	6	8	4	
		4	2	3		7	1	
	8	3	5	6	1		9	4
2	1			7		5		3
							7	8
		8	9		2	1	3	5
	3		8	5	7	4		2

	8		2	6	4	3	1	
3		2	1	9	8		4	6
4	6	1	7	5	3	2		
9	1			7	6		2	3
		7	8				6	
	4	8				7	9	1
					1	6		2
7	9			4	2	1		
1	2	6	5	8			3	

	4		6			1	8	
		1	2					9
5		2			1	3	4	
8		4	1		6			3
9		6				8	7	1
1	3		7	9	8	6		
2			4	1		9	6	
3		7	9		2	4	1	
4					7	2	3	

8	7		2	5			4	1
6		1		7	8	5	9	
	9	5					8	
5				9	2			4
1	3	2			4		7	9
	8		1	3		2		
		6	4		5		1	7
7		8	9			4	6	
	5			1	6	9	2	8

6	9	4			3		1	8
1	7	8			2	5		3
2		3			1	7	6	
			3	7	6			
		2	4	1	9			7
7	6		5		8		4	1
5	2		8	3		9		
3		6	2	9		1		5
	8			6	5		3	

	5	6	2	7	8	1	4	
2	4	3				8	5	7
	8		3		4	9		6
6	9				7			5
3			9	8	1			
	7	8	5		6	2		9
5		4	8	1			9	2
					2		6	1
		2	6	9		4	3	8

	1	4		5			9	6
9					6	2	1	4
6	2		9					5
	6	2	5	8			4	1
1			6	9			8	
	8	9	4	3		6	5	
	7			2	5			9
			7	6	8			3
2		6						8

	2	9	5		1	8	4	
1			4	3	8	7	2	
7	4	8	6			5	3	1
4	5			9				
8		1		4		9	5	
	9	3	7			4		2
5			9		2		7	
2	8	7				1	9	5
9	3			5		2	6	

7		9		4		8	5	2
	5			7	2			
	4			8	1		6	
4				2			9	5
5	9	8	7		4			1
3	6			9	5	4		
		5				9	1	8
		4	6			2		3
	3	7	2		8	5		

	7	1				3	4	5
8	4		9			1		
	3				7		9	2
7			5	6		9	3	1
3		9				6	5	
	8	6	3	1	9		7	
4	6	7		9	1	5	2	
	5	3		2	4	7		9
		8		3		4		6

	1	4	6	7	8	3		9
9		6				4		
3	2	8		4	1	6		
2	9						5	
4	6					1		3
7		1	5			2		4
			7	8	6		4	2
6		7			2		3	8
	4			9			1	

	1	7						3
		4				5	8	
	8		1		5	7	9	4
		5	8				3	2
			4		7	8		9
		8	5	3	2		1	7
4	7		6	5			2	
		3		4	8	9		
8			7	1	9		4	6

		4	5			2	7	
	8		1		9		4	3
9	7		4					
	9		8				2	
	4	2			7	8	1	5
8			3	5	2		9	7
1	2		7	8	3		6	4
4	5	8		6	1			2
7			2	4			8	1

9		7	5	6			3	2
8		1	9			4	5	6
	3			2	4			
	1	2	3	9	7		6	
6	9			1	8	7	4	3
				5	6		1	
	6				2		8	
2		4	1		5	6		
		3		8		1	2	4

			3		8		4	
4	3		2	6	9			
8				4	7		6	2
	8			2		5		7
7		4		1	5			6
	1		7			9	2	4
	7	6	8	9	1		5	
3		8	5					1
9				3			7	8

	1		7	5		3	8	
7		9		8		2	5	
	6				9	1		
	9		8	6		5	1	
	5	3			2		7	
1	8	2		9		6		
9	4					7	2	1
3	7		2		1		9	
					5	4	6	

	1	8	9			6		2
	2		1	8		4	9	3
	9	6	2		4		5	8
6						9	2	1
		9		1	2			4
1	8			6		7	3	
	3		7	9	1		4	6
			5		8	3	1	7
2	7	1			3	5		9

2			3		9	7	4	
					6	1		8
7	1	6			4	5		
5	7	4		3	1	6		
	6	2		4		9	5	3
	8	3	2		5	4	1	
	2				3			
6	9		4					
		5	1	9	7	2	6	4

5			4		1	9	6	
2		1		9		7		3
		4	3	2	7		8	
4					3			
			1	4		3	5	6
6	1	3	8	5			2	
					5	2	9	
7	9	8	2	6			3	1
3	2		9	1	8		7	4

2	7				3		5	
5					9			
9	3		5		4	6	7	1
	9	7	2			5	4	3
	2	5	7	4	8	1		
	1		9	3			8	7
	5					8		
7		9		8	2			
4		2	3	5			1	9

5	6	8	7		4			
	7		1			8	4	5
4	3		5			6		
6	9		4	3			5	7
	5	3		7	1	4	2	9
1			9		2			
3		6			5			8
9	8	5		1	7		6	
		4	8	9	6			3

7	1					3	5	9
2	6		3	4	9	7	8	
9		8				6		2
	7	9		8			1	5
5	4		2		6	9	7	
		2						6
		7				5	6	4
8				9			2	3
4	2						9	7

		6			8	9	1	4
3		1		5	7			2
				4		3		5
7		2	4		5			9
4	1				2	7		
6	5			7	3		4	
8	6	5	3		9	4		7
	9	7			4		6	
	3		7		6	5	9	

4	5		7			3		2
6	2	3	5			7	8	1
		9			8		6	
	1				9		5	
	9	6		5	7	4	1	3
		5	4	1		6		
8		2		7	6			5
	3	7		8	2	1	4	
			3	4	5			8

		7		2	8	1	5	3
		3	4	7			8	2
		1	5	9	3			
3		8			9			1
5			1		2	3		
1			3	6			2	
7		2	9			8		
		5	8	4	7		3	6
8		4		3			1	

				1	9		5	2
2	4	5	7	6	3	9		1
	1			5	4			
	9				5		1	
5		8				7	4	6
		1	4			5		9
	6	2	3			1	7	5
7	5	4	1		6		2	
	8	3		7	2	6	9	

	1				5		9	7
	6	5	3	8	7		1	2
7	3			1	2	8	5	
4	2		7	3	1			
	5		8	2			4	3
	9	1	6		4			8
		3		7	6		8	9
1		6			3	7		4
5	7		2	4				1

2	7	5		3	4		9	1
1		9	8	7		3	4	2
		3				5		
9		2	4					
		7		6			8	9
3	8	6		9		4	2	5
	9					2		
5	3		1	2	7	9		
		4			9			3

	5	6	9				7	1
3				1				9
9	1			8	6	4	3	2
	7	3				5	1	4
		1	3		4	7	9	
6	9		7	5				8
7	4	2			3	1		5
1	6	5	2		8	9	4	
	3			4				

9	4		5		3	8	7	
		2	8		1		9	3
3		8	9	7	2			4
4	2		7	1	5	3		
1	7	9				4		
		3			6			7
		7	6			9	2	1
6				2		7	4	
	9		1	8		6		5

			6	4	1	3	8	5
6	3	1			7		4	2
			3		2			7
2	9			3		7		6
	4			6	5	8		
3		6		7	8	4	9	1
5	1	9		8	6	2		
8	2				3	6	7	9
7		3		2	9	5		

	2				3		8	7
	4		7				2	3
			9	2	8		5	
2	5		4			8		
9			2		7		1	4
			1		9	2	6	5
4					5		3	2
1	3	2		7	4	5		
8				9	2	7		

5	4	7	8		9		6	1
		3	4	7		5		
2	9	8	5	6			7	
	8	6	7	1			3	
7	1	2			3		5	
9	3		2			1		
		1	6	2		7		8
6	7	4	1			3		5
	2		3	5		6	1	4

4	7	3			8	1	9	6
		5	4	7			8	3
	9	8	1	6	3		4	
	5		7	8	6	3		4
	4	7	5					9
	2		9	4	1	7		
1			8		7			5
	3	2					7	
7	8				5	4		2

		2	9	4		7	6	3
	9		8		7	5		1
6	5		1		3	9	8	
		6	3	1				
2		8		5	4	3		9
5	3	9	2	7		1	4	6
3					2	4		5
	2		4	3		8		
		4			1	6	3	2

	8	1	7		5	2		4
	4	3	1	8	2	7		
	5	7	9	3		6	1	
4				2	6			3
8					3	4		2
3	6				9	5		
		8	3	4			2	6
		4	6	5	8		9	
	3	6	2	9	1	8		5

7					2			
5			9			6		3
6		2	1	4			9	8
1			2	3	9	4	8	5
		5	7				1	
8	9	3				2		6
	7		5		4		3	1
3	1	4		9			6	2
2	5	8	6	1	3		4	7

		4		8		6		1
6	3		7	5		8		9
8		1	9	6	4	3		2
3		9			5			
4	6	8	3		2	7		5
2	7		4		6	9		
			1	4	7			6
				3				7
	4	7				1		8

	6				8	9	1	5
		9	2	6	5	4	3	7
		4		9	1	6	8	2
		7	1		6		9	8
	8			5			2	1
1	3		9					
	9	8	6	4		1		
5		3	8			2		4
		1	5	2			7	9

1			3		6		2	4
4	9	2			1	6	8	3
	7	6	4	2		5	1	9
	4						9	2
	6	5	2	1		3		7
9			7				5	6
		4				9	7	5
		7	9		4	2	3	8
2	3	9				4	6	

2		9	4		5			7
3	6	4	8	2	7		5	
5	1	7	6		3	8	2	
		3		4	6	2		1
9		8			2	5		
	2	6		5	8			3
	7	1	2	8				
4	3	2	5	6			1	8
	9			7		4		2

2				9	8	1	7	
8	7	5	2			6	9	
9		1			7	5	2	8
1	5	2			4		8	6
7	9		1	8			5	2
4				5		9	1	
5	4	8	7					1
			4		5	8	6	
	2	9	8		1	7	4	5

2			6		5	9	7	
1	5	6				4		8
7	3		4	8		2		
			1	4	2	5	8	7
5			9	6	8		2	
4		2	3	5	7		6	9
8				2	6	7	1	3
			7	9	3	8		5
				1	4	6		2

2			5			3		1
	1		8	3		2		4
4			2	1	7			5
	6	7	1	5			3	9
		2			3		1	7
9	3	1	7					6
7	2	9			5	1	4	
3	8			7	1		5	
1	5				8		6	3

	8		3	2		9	1	
7	3	1			9		4	8
4	2	9	1			6		5
		2	9		7		6	
	7	8	4		6		5	
3	6		2	1		7	8	9
	4	3			1	5	2	
		5			3	4		
6		7			2			

	8			6	7	5	9	2
6		9	1		5	3		
2				8	4	6	7	
8			6	9			3	
			4		8	2		6
4		6		1		8	5	9
7		2			9	1		
	4	1	8	3	6	7		
5		8		7	1	9	6	4

		2	3	8		5		
8	3	9					2	
		7	2		6	9		
2					1			9
9	7	1		2	3			
		5			7	6	1	2
					4	3	9	7
	5	3	9	7		1		8
7		6		3	8	2	5	

2	1		9	4	3			6
6			2	1	8	7	9	
				7		2		3
1		2	3	6	5	9	4	7
		6	8		7	1		2
		9				6	3	
		3		8		4		1
		8					2	
7					9	8	6	5

7	4	2		6	8		3	5
	1	3			2	6		
	6		5		7	4	1	2
		5	7	2			6	
	9		8	1			2	
		4		5	6		9	
9		1				7		
				7	1	3	5	9
3		6		8	5			

1		5	4	7		3	9	6
2		4	3				8	
6		3		1			7	4
8	3		9	4	5		6	
4		6	8		7	5	1	9
7		9		2	6		4	3
5		7						8
	4	8	7					1
3	1		6	8		9	5	7

	9	8	6	2			5	
					9		8	2
2		1	5	8		9		3
4		5			2	8	7	9
8	3	2	7		4			
			1		8		2	
9			2					5
	5				3	2		8
7	2			4	5	6	9	1

	6	7	4	2	3		5	
		8		7		9		
4	5		9		8		7	
3		6	1			7		8
	7	2						
	9			8	4	3		6
	2	4			5	1		
	3	5		6		2	4	9
		9		4	1	5		3

7	8		6	9		4	1	
		3	2					6
	6		7	3	1		9	8
9			4	8	3		6	2
2			1		6		4	
6	1			2	9	3		7
5		9	8	1			3	
				5		9	2	1
	4	1	9				7	5

	2			8	9			5
		5			4	3		6
9	1		6	5	3	7	8	
		8	9	7			2	1
7				6		8	3	9
	9			3		4		7
				2				8
5	3	7	1		8		6	
	8	1	5	4		9	7	

	7	8	3				2	
1					4	5	8	7
4	6	2		5		9		3
6	5			3	8	2	7	
2		4	7	9	6		5	
9	8		1		5		4	
7		9	5		3	4		
8		6		4		7	3	
		5						2

	4	9		8		5	2	3
7	6			2	5		4	1
2		3	9	4		8		
5			8	1		2	3	9
3	8	2			9		1	
			7		2	6	5	8
		5		9		1		
6		1	4		8		9	5
				5		4		2

	8		4	6				
9	7	2	3	8		4	5	6
	6	3				8		1
	5		1	3				
7	2				6			8
	4				8	9	6	
2	3	8		9				
5	1		6	2	4		8	9
			8	1		5	2	7

	1	3	6			5	4	2
4	2			1	5	9		
	5							
			4		3	1		5
5	9		2					6
		1	8	5	9		2	
3	7			4		2		9
9	6	2			7			1
1	4		9	3	2	8	6	7

9	2		3			1		5
5	7			8	1			4
4				6	5	3		
		9			4			
6		8		5	9	4	2	3
7	5		8	2	3	9	6	1
3	6	7	4	9			1	8
		2		3			4	6
		5			6	2	3	

		7	9	8	3	4	6	5
	8			7		3		
9	3	4	6	5	2	1		7
4	9	1		3	6	2		8
		8		2	1	9	3	
	2			9	8			4
						6	2	
		2	8	6		7		3
	6	5	2	1		8	4	

5	2		4	8		6		
8			9		3	2	5	7
	6	3	7	2		8		4
2	9				7	1	8	
4		8			9			5
	3	5	6			4	9	2
6	7	9	1		4	3	2	
	5	2	8	7			4	
		4			2		7	

	5		9	1	2	3	8	7
9	1		3		7	6	4	
	3	8		5	4	9		1
				2	3	4	7	
3	2				8		5	9
	4		1		9	2	3	6
	8		2		5			
	6	4	7					
2		3				5	1	

	9				8	6		1
6	8			3	4	5	7	2
		7		1	2	3	9	
4	2	8		6	1	9		5
	5				3	7		
		3		9			2	
		4	1		9		6	7
		5			6		8	9
		9	2	8				

3			8	6	4		1	
7	4	6		2			5	
8		9	7		5	2	4	6
		4	5	8		6		7
1		8	2	7			9	
6	7	5		4			8	2
								1
2		1			8		7	4
		3	4					8

	3	2	4	7				
9	4	7	8	1	6	5	2	
8			3	5		4	7	9
3	7	4				6		1
2		1		8	3			
6	8	9			7	2	3	5
	6	3	2	9				
7					4			2
	2				1			8

8					2	9	3	6
6				3	1	8		
2		4	8	9	6			1
1		5	3		8	4	7	9
7		2	4	5	9	6	1	
	4		6		7		8	5
4				8	5	3		7
		6	1	7		5	2	
5		8			3	1		4

		3		1	7		9	4
7			6			8	1	2
	1	5			8			6
5	3	6		7	9	4		
4		8	3		2	1	5	9
			5	8		3	6	
1	4	2			5	6		3
6	8	9					7	
3	5			2		9		1

3		8	1		5			
2	1				6			4
	9			2		5	1	8
		3	9				7	
7	8				3	4	2	
		9	8		2			5
		2		1		6		
9	3	4	2	6		7	5	1
	5		4	3	7		8	2

2	3		4	5				8
5		6		9				3
8	4		3	6		1		
3	9	5		7		8		6
7	1	8			6			4
	6				5		3	7
9		7		8			4	
1					3	5		
6	2			4	9	7		

8			9	3	6	5		7
	9	6	5	8		1	2	
	7						8	9
	3			2	9			5
		9	3			4	6	
7		2	4	6		3	9	
2	4	7	6		8	9	3	1
			7	1	3	2	5	
	5	3	2	9	4	8		

9		1	4	2	6			3
			7	9	1	2	8	
				5	3	6	9	1
6	4	5			8			2
3			6	1			4	
2	1			7	4	3		
8	6	3	2	4	9	1		7
	5	9		6	7	4	2	8
		4	1	8				

	5	1	6		7			
8		7	5		1			6
6		4	2		3	7		1
		8		6				4
		2	1	3	8	9	6	5
	1			7	5	8	3	
1	8	9	3	5	6	2		
4		5	8	2				3
2		3	7			5	8	

4	7			9				3
3				2	4		1	5
						4		
9	3			8	5		6	
	2	6					5	8
	8			3		1	9	7
7	9		2	1	8	5	4	6
2	5				6		3	
6		1	3				7	2

6	8	5	1	7	3	2		
2	1	4	5	6			3	7
		3	8		2	5	6	1
5	6	1	3		4			
		7			6		5	3
	2							4
4		2			1		7	
9		6	4	2				
	5	8			7		2	

	4		9	2	1	5	6	3
	3	9		5	6			2
6			3	4	7		8	9
		3			4	9	2	
		1		6	8			
2		4	5		3	7		8
4		5		8			3	7
	1	8	6	7		2	9	
7	9	6	4		2	8		1

5	4				8	2	1	6
1	8	2		7		4	9	
		9		1	4		8	5
	1		8	9	5	3	2	
2	5					8		9
		4		2		6	5	1
	7				9		3	2
		5	4	8	3	1	6	7
3	6		7		2	9		

			3	8	6		9	
	9		1			4	3	
3	1		5		9		2	7
4	5	1	8	3	7		6	2
7	3			6		8	1	4
	6	2	9	1		5		3
5					1	7		6
1	8	7				2	4	
			7	2		3	5	1

1	9	6	4		2		5	
		4	7		8		1	
	7		6	1		4	2	
6						9	3	
4		8	3		9		7	
			8	7	1	5	6	
2		5		4	6	7	9	
	6			8	7			1
7	4		9		3			5

9				2			8	
7	8		3	9	5	2	6	4
	4				6		9	
	5	3		4	2			1
1	7	2		5		3		6
6	9	4	7				5	2
	6	7			9	4	1	
3					4			7
4	2		1	6			3	9

		1	6			7	9	
9	6	2		1	5		3	
		3	2					
6	2	5		7	1	8		3
1	3	9				5	2	7
4	8	7					6	
	9		3	4	2	1		
	7	6	1	5	9	2		4
2	1				7		5	

9	4		5	3		7		6
	6		4	7		1	8	
		5				4		
	5			4				3
			8				7	
	3	7	2		6		4	8
7							1	2
5	1	3	9	2	4		6	7
		6		8	1		5	4

9						6	5	4
		3	5					7
	5	7	2	9		8		3
4	3	9						
7		5	1			4	6	8
1	8			4	5	3	2	9
	9	8				5	4	
5	6		9	8	2	7	3	1
2		1	4	5	3	9		6

5	7	1	4		6		2	8
	6	3	8		2	4		
4	8			1	9	7	3	
				4	5	8	9	1
	5	8	2			6		
7	9	4			8			2
	4	9		2			8	
	3			8	7			9
8			9					3

7	2		9	8		3	5	6
	6				5	2		
1	9			3				4
	3	6	5	7			9	
			8	6			2	
9		8					7	5
		2	4		8		3	
3	7	1	2			9	4	8
4	8		3		7	5	6	

6		5	2	1	4			
4		1	9	8				6
8			6	5	7	4	9	
		4	8		6		7	
				3		8		
	8		4		2	6	1	5
	3	8	7	2	9	1	6	
2					1			8
							3	7

	2	6	5	4	8	3		
3	8			6	7	2	5	
7	9		2		3	4		
2						8		
6		8		9		7		3
4	3		7	8		1	6	5
	6	3	8	7	1			
	1					6	3	
9	4	7				5		8

1	8	3	2					9
6	2		1		9			
		5			6	1	8	
8	6			5				
	7		6			5		8
5	9	1	8	2	7		4	6
4			5		2		6	7
2	1	6			3		5	4
			4		8	2	1	3

1	8	4	5	2	7	9	6	
9				4	1	7		2
		2		9		8	1	4
3			4		8	5	2	6
6					2	3		
2	5	8	6					
7		3	1	8	4			5
8			2	3		4	7	
		5	7	6	9	2	3	8

	2	6	1		8	7		5
9	3			4		1	8	
	7		3		5	4	6	9
6		3	8	7			5	
5				6			7	
		2		5	3			
3	5		2	1	9		4	8
1				3		9		7
	4	9	6	8	7		1	

		1					7	8
2	6	8	1	4		3	5	
7		9		8		4		
9	2	6	5	3				7
3	5	7	9		8	6	4	2
8	1	4			6			3
		2		5		8	1	6
	8	3	4			9		5
1			8	6	2	7		4

3				4	2	7	6	8
				3	7	5	1	
7	1				5			3
6	3	9			8	1	5	7
5		8					9	2
	4	1		5	9	8	3	
	2		5		4	6	7	1
1					3	9	8	4
8		4	9		1		2	5

	5		7		9			
4		3		1	5	8		
	7		3	4		9		
		2	4			3	6	5
5	8	4	9	6	3		2	1
3	6		5	2	1		8	
	4			3	2	6	9	8
1	2	8			7	5	4	3
		9						7

2	4		3		8		9	7
	9	7	4		5		3	
3	8	5		7			6	4
9	6		5	3	7	4		1
			2	8	6	7		
			1		9		2	6
	3		8	2		9		5
				5		8	7	
	5		7	9	3	6		

	3	5	2			1	4	
	4	7	1	8		2	3	
		2	7	4		8	6	5
5	7	6			2	9		4
2			8	6	9		7	3
9			4	5	7		1	
7		9			8	4		
	2		5	7	1			6
		1			4			

5		3		1	2		7	9
	6	7		3	8			
			4			3	2	6
			2	9	3	7		
1	8	9	7	5	6	2	4	3
7	3		1	8		9		5
4			8	2		6		7
8	7	6	3		9	1		
	2		5			4		

6		3		9	1		8	5
	8		2		5	1	3	9
		9	3	8	7		6	2
		4	5		6	9		
	1	2		4	8	6	5	3
			1			2		
	4	8			9	3	1	7
				1		5	9	4
5			7		4		2	

5	9	6	4	3		2		
4		8					5	7
7	2		8	1			9	4
9	5							
3				7		9	2	
				9	1	5		3
1		5	3		6		8	9
6	7			8	9			5
8	3	9	7			1		2

7	6					4	1	
3	4	1		6		2		9
		9	4		1		3	7
1						9	6	2
6	9			7	2		4	5
	3					7		1
9			8		4			
			5			8	9	
2	8		9	1		5	7	

	8	1	2			7		
7	5						2	
4			8	3	7	6	1	5
		4	5					
2	9	8		4	6		7	
5	7			1	2		8	6
8	4	2			1	3	6	9
9		5		8	3	2	4	
6	3	7	4		9	1		

3		4	5	9	6		8	
9	2			1	8	4		
			3			9	1	6
8		1	2	4	3	5	7	
4	3	9		5			2	1
7				6			4	8
1	9			7	2	8		
2		5	4			1		
6	4		1	3		2	9	7

	2	1					5	9
3			9	8	5		6	
	9	6		2	7			8
	8				2	1		5
			5	4				3
1	7	5	3	9				
	1	2	4				8	
9		4	8	7		5	1	2
7	5	8	2	1		4		6

3	5		9		6			2
8			1		4		5	
4		2		8	5			
	2		7	1		6		
1		7		6	3	2	9	5
	4	3	2	5		8		1
9	6	5		3		1	2	
			5		1		6	7
7		4	6	9		5	3	8

2	5	1	8		4	9		7
	6	7			9	2	4	1
9	3	4	7		1		6	
6	7	5	2	1	8			
3		9	6	4	5			2
1				7				5
5	2	8					7	
4	1	6	3		7		2	9
7				8		4		6

	1			8		2	9	
5	9	8	7	2	6	3	4	
	2	3		1		5	6	8
2	4		8		9	1	5	6
	5		4	7	1	8		
	8	9		5			7	
9	3		5	4		6	8	2
8			2		3	7	1	
	7			6				5

6					3	2	4	1
2		9		8		7	6	
7		4	5			9		3
1		7					2	6
		2		6			5	
3	6		7			8	1	9
		3	6	1		5		2
	2		4				3	
	8		2		9	6		

5	6	2		1	3		9	
	7				5	6	3	
4	1	3	9					2
6	9		3	8		2	4	5
					9	1		8
8	2			7	4			3
		6		9		3	5	
1	4	5		3		8		9
				5		7	1	

		1		9				
6	3	4	7	1				8
		7		3		4		
7	2	5		6		1	9	
				7		2	8	
	1			5	3	6	7	
5			1	2	7		4	
1	9			4	6			2
4	7		5	8	9			6

5		1	2	7	8		9	3
	2			1			5	6
		3	5	6	9			
6	4	2	9	8			3	
	9			4				
	1			3			2	4
2	8		4	5	1		6	
9	5			2	3	8	4	1
1	3	4	8				7	

3	7	2	9					
5	6	4		7	2		9	3
	9	8		5				7
9	8	3	4	2			6	5
7	4			6	9	3	8	
2	5				8	9	4	1
	3	9	2	8	7	5	1	4
				4	5		3	
			6			2	7	8

	1		3	8				
	4		2	9			6	
	5	2	1	6		8		7
		3	9	2		6	5	1
	9		4			3	7	2
2	6							
6	2		8	7	3	4	1	5
1	8	7	5	4	9	2	3	6
5		4	6			7		9

	3	5	6	7		8		2
2		4		5	3	9	6	7
7	9	6	2			3	5	
			4					5
	2			1		4		3
	4	9	5	8	2	1		
6		3	8	9			2	4
	7		3	6	4			
4		8	7	2	5	6	3	9

	6		2	3	9			
8	2						4	
5			8	4		3	2	6
4		1	5	8				9
			4	7		8	6	1
2	8			9		7	5	
6		7			5		8	2
9			3	6	8		7	5
1	5		7		4			

2	6				8			
5	9		1				6	8
3	7	8		4	6	9	1	
	5	3		2	9	1	8	
4	8			5			2	
1				8				6
7	1	6				8		
	3			1		6	4	
9	4			6	5	7		

6				1	7	8		4
	4		8	5	9		6	
	1	9	4	6		7		2
9			7			1	4	5
4	3		9		1		7	6
7	2					9		3
5		2	3		4	6	1	
	7			9	5		2	
1	9	4	6	2	8			7

7	9			5	1		3	
				6	3		2	9
	6	1	4	9	2		5	
4			9	8	6			2
9	1	5	3					4
		6			4	9		3
6	2	3	1	4		8		
1	7	9		3	8			
	5	4	2	7		3	6	

							4	1
	5	1			6	3	9	8
8	9	6		3	1			
5	1	8				4	2	
6								7
2			3			5		6
	4		7	2	3		6	9
		2	5			1	7	
	6		1	4	8	2	3	5

		5	2				3	6
9	8			3	5	1		
6	3	2	9		7		8	
1	5			6	3	2		4
							5	
2	6	7		5	1	8		3
				2	6			
	2	6	5		8	3		
3	7	8	1					2

	7	8			9		4	
3			5	4	7		8	
		4	1	2		7		3
				5	1	8	2	
		1	7	3		9	6	5
		2	4		6			7
7		5			4	6	3	2
					5			
	8	6			3	1	5	9

1	9	8	7	3	2	5		6
2		5	9				8	
4	6		5			9	2	
7			2		4	6		
	1	4				2		8
9	2						3	
		9		1			7	2
3	5	2				1	6	4
			4	2				9

6	3	5				7		9
	1		6	9				5
	7	9	5	1	3	8		
		3					6	1
	9				6	2	7	
	8	6	2	7	1			
				3	8		5	
3	4	7				6	8	2
			4			9	3	7

		2	7	6				9
7		1	8	9	2		3	
9	3	6		5		2		8
8	9	3					2	4
	4	5		7	8	3	9	1
2	1				9	8		
		4	9	3	1		8	7
		9	4	8			1	2
1	6	8			7			3

2			4	7	9	8	5	3
			1	5	8	2	6	9
		9					7	4
3					5	9	4	
9	6	4	2	8	7	3	1	5
1				3				7
8		2	7	9		4		1
7	4				3	5	9	
6	9	3			1	7	2	

9		1	3	4	7	6	2	
				6			7	1
3		7	1	2		9	4	8
8	3		6	5				
5		9	4					
1	2	6	7	3	9	5	8	
2		5	8				1	6
	4	3	2		6	8		9
6		8	5	9		2		

1	6	4	5		8			7
7		2	4	9			6	1
		3	1	7	6	2	8	4
5							7	
3		9	6	5	1		4	
8		1	2		7		9	
	9	7		1		4	2	8
	3	5	9			7	1	6
2	1	8					5	

9		3		8	2	5	1	
8			9				4	3
	5		1	4		2	8	
	6	8	7	5			3	
		9	8			4	5	
		5		2		9		8
			2			8		
	8	4		6	7	3	9	
5					8	7		4

					9	5		3
6	3				7		9	4
9	4		1		6		2	
3	5		7				4	
8	7	2	9	1		6		
1	9		5	6		8		2
4	1		6					7
						4	1	
2	6	7		4	1	3	5	9

	4	7	8		9		1	
					2		8	
8			3	4		9		6
	8		7	2	1	5	6	9
5					6		4	
	1	9				8		7
2			6	9	7	1	5	8
		8		5	3		9	2
7			2	1		6	3	4

8		9	6	2	3		4	
	6							7
	5	2	7	4	9		6	
2	4	6	3		1	7	5	9
	3	8		5	6	2		
					4			
	2			6			9	
5		4			2	6		3
			4	3	5	1	8	

6	1		8	4	2	9		3
4			9			8		
		9	7		6		5	1
		6	2	8	4	3	1	5
2	4			5		7	8	
5	8			7	1		9	
9		2	4		7	1		8
3				9				7
1						6		

		8	9				4	5
4	5	9					7	1
6	7	1	5			9		
7		3		6			8	2
8	4			2		1	6	
	6	2	4		8	5		7
			8				1	
	8	6	3	1	4	7		
9	1				7			

2								
7				2		8	5	3
5	6	8			1	4	2	7
3	8	6			9	5	1	
9		2	1	6		7		
4			3			6	9	8
1		3			4			5
6	4			8		9		1
	2		5				4	

2		6	3	9		5		4
7	5			2	1	9		8
1				8	5		3	
8	6	7		4	3			
4			9	7		6	8	3
3					6	7	4	
	7		1		4	3	9	2
6					9			
	2		7		8			

	8			9		1	6	7
9	3		8	6			4	2
		1	2				9	3
	1	9			4	3	2	6
7	4	5		3		9	1	8
		3	9	1		7	5	
1					3	6	7	
	7	8	1			2		9
					9			1

	2	3		9	8		7	1
	5			4		3	8	
	1	4				9	5	
	8	6	2					4
3			8	6	4		9	
	9				5	8	6	
	4	7		8	6		1	3
1			4	5	7			
9	6	5	1	3	2			

	4	5		7				9
3	2	9	1	5	8	7		
8	7	6	3		4			
6		7	8	3			2	
	3	4	6	1	2			7
2			5	4	7			3
5	8		9	6		1	7	4
			4	8	1	2	9	
4		1		2				

7		5				8	3	
	2			9		1		4
		6			3		5	7
	3		6	1		4	8	5
1		4	5	2		6	9	
			8		4			
5		1		6				8
8		3	4		1	2		
9	4		3		8	5		6

		1			3			6
4	9	7	8			2		5
3			4	5	7		9	1
					8		2	
2	1		6		9	5	7	8
				4	2	3		9
	4	2						
	3	9	7	6			8	2
1	7	8	2	9		6	5	3

2	3		6	5			9	4
6			8			3	2	
8	4	9	3	2		6		
4	2	6	7		8	5		9
3	5		9		4		6	8
1	9		2		5			
			1			9	8	
7	8	2			6	1		5
		3	5			7	4	

		4	9	6	1	7		
7				3			4	
1	6	8		5	4	2	9	3
2		1	5			3	6	
6			3		2	4		1
4	5	3	8		6	9		
8	4	6		9		5	2	
9	1		6	2		8		4
		2			7	6		9

4	5		9		1	8		
	3	7			6	9	5	4
8	9		5		4	1		3
3	8	5			7	2		9
		4	3				8	5
	1	9			8			
5	4	8				6		7
9	7			8	2	5		
6			7	4				8

1	2	6		7	8			
5		7		3	1		8	6
9		8	4		2	5		7
3		5	7		4		2	
8	1	2	3	9	6			5
7		4				6		1
			8			1		3
6				5		4		
4	7		6	2	3	8		9

			8	5			9	
						4		
4	6	7	1	2	9	8	5	3
				1		2	6	8
1	5	2	7	8			3	
		8		3	2		7	5
	4	6		7	1		2	9
2					8	5	4	
	1	9	2	4		6		

		8	1	5			2	3
9	2					1	7	
	1	4		9	7	8		6
		3	7	2		6	1	
	9	6	3	1	8		4	2
			6	4		3		
2	6	1	5			4		
4	8			6				
5	3	9	4	8				

6			1	5		7		
1				4	9	6	5	
4	3		2					8
9	4	6	5	8				7
		3	4	7	6		8	
			9	3	2		4	6
3	5	1	7					2
			6	2	5		9	
	6		3	1	8		7	5

	6				2	7		5
7				5	8	2	4	
		5	7	9	4			
1	7	2	4		3	5		
	9	3			1	4	2	6
	4	6	2		9	3		
6		4		3		9	1	
9	5	8		2	7			4
3	1	7		4				

2	6	4						3
7			2		5	8	6	4
	8	5		6	3		2	
1		7	9	4		2		5
	9				8	4	3	7
5	4			3	2			6
	2		5	8			7	9
4			6		7	3		
8	7	6					4	

	8	2	4	3	6	1		
		3	5	9		4	6	
	9			2	7		5	3
4			3	5		2	8	7
8	2		9	7	4		3	
	3	1	6					5
3	1	8	2	6	5	7		4
			7	1	3		2	
	5						1	6

	2			4	7		1	
4	8	1	2		5	7		
5		7	9		8		2	
8	6	5		2	3	1		4
	9	4	6		1			3
1	7		4			6	8	2
		8	1			2	5	7
		6	8	7	2	9		1
7		2	5					8

			6		3	4	8	5
		8		1	5	6	9	3
3	5	6	9		8			7
5		3	4			8		
	8	1	5	9				
	2			8	1	7		4
2	3			5			4	
1				3				
	9		7		4	3	6	1

		9						2
2			7	3		9	8	1
	1	7			9	5	4	6
1	7	5		4	3	2	9	8
8	3							4
6		4	5			7		3
9	6		2			4	3	
5	2		4		7	8	6	
7	4		3			1	2	5

1	2			4				5
	3	7	5	1	8	4		6
	6	4	2	3	9	8		
	8					3	5	2
			8			6		9
6	1	5	9					
8		1	3	5		2	6	4
	7	6	4	8			9	3
4				9		1	8	7

7	2	9		1	4			
6			2	9	5			
	4	5	8			2		9
5		7			6	1	2	3
4		2				5	9	
	6		5		9	4	7	
2	3		9	7	8			
9	5		1	4				2
	7				2		3	4

					7			5
5	9	3	2	1	6	7	8	
	7	2					9	3
		9					7	
7		1	8					9
	5	8		6	9		2	1
8	1	7		5		9		2
		5	4	7			3	8
		6	9		2	5	1	

	4			8		1		6
			4		3		5	2
5		2	6	7		3		8
	7	6			4	9		
	5	4	3	2			6	7
8		1					2	4
1		5						9
4	6		1	9		2	7	
	9	7		4	8			5

2	4			9		3	7	5
		7	3			1	8	
9	3	1			7	2	6	4
6	8	9		7	3	4	2	1
		3	4		9	7	5	
7			1		2		9	3
	9	2		1				
			2			9		
4	7	5		3		6	1	2

2	8		6	4				9
	7	5						6
	3	6	5		1	2	4	8
	9			2				5
1			9	8		6	7	3
7					5	4	9	2
6			2	5	7			1
				6		5	2	4
5		9		1	8		6	7

1	2	9	3			7		5
3		6	1	8	5	2		
			9			3		1
			2			4	1	8
7	4		8	9	1	5		
6	1	8					7	2
4		3		2	8	1	9	7
2		1	7				5	4
5	9	7	6	1				3

	3	7		2	4	1	5	
6	1	2	7	8				
	5	8	9			2	7	6
8				9				7
5			3	4		8	1	2
2		3	1	5		6	9	
3	6		8	1	9			5
7	2		5	6		4	8	
		5	4	7	2	3		

		4	5		2		1	6
2			4	9		5		8
5	6	8					2	4
6	4		1	5	7	3	8	9
		3	9	6		1		2
		9			4	6	7	
	9	5	7	2		8	6	1
3	1		8				5	
8	2	7		1	5	4		

			5				4	
5		4		9		8	3	1
3	7		1			5	9	2
	4	7		3	9		5	8
2	9			1			6	
8		6	4		2		7	
4	1	2	3					
6		9	8			3	2	4
	8	3			4	6	1	

	1		3		2	7	4	5
		6						
	3	2				1		6
9	6	1	2			4		
2				9	5	6		1
3		8	4			9	2	7
7	8	5			9	2	1	4
1	2		7		8	5	6	9
6	9		5		1	8	7	3

9	8		2					
7		4	9	3		2		
					5		7	
1	7	6			9	4	3	
3	4	9		1			2	
	2	8		6	3			7
4		3		5	7	8	9	
	1	7		9	2		5	
2				8			6	

3	2	6						
			2		8		9	5
	9		4		7		1	6
4	1	9	7	5	6	8		
						4		7
	6		3	2		9		1
		2		7		1		8
6		7	8			5	4	
	8		9		3	6	7	

6	2	5	9	7	4	8		
	8	4	2		3		7	6
			6	5	8	9	4	
	5	2	1	9	6	4		
	4	6	8					
8	1	9	4		5	2		
4		1				7		5
	9		7	4	2		8	1
	7	8	5					4

		3			1		4	2
5	1	8				3		9
	6		3			1	8	
		9		4				
6	2		8	9	3	5	1	4
8			1	2		9	3	6
		1	7		6			
7	8	6		1	4		5	3
	9	4		5	8	7	6	

1				6	8			3
	6	8		2		9	5	1
	5	3			9	8		2
	2			3			8	
	7	1		8	2	3	4	9
8		6		7		2		
	1	9	7			5		
3		7	2		6		9	4
			8	9	1	6		

	2						1	
8	1	3					5	
6		4	3	9	1			
2	6	9		7	3	1	4	5
7	3	1		4		2	9	
	8	5		1		7		
1	4				2	9	8	7
3		2		8	7	5	6	4
		8		6	4	3		1

	7			9			5	4
				7	6	2	9	8
		6		2	5			
4	5		8	1		9		6
2			5	6				
1			7	3	9		4	
6	4	3				8		9
9	8	5		4	7	1	2	
	2	1	9		3			5

	7	5	9		6	3	1	
		3		4		7	6	8
6	8		3		2	4		9
	6	2	8	3		1	7	4
8	5	4	1	2			3	6
1	3	7	4	6	9			
				5				1
7		9			4	5	8	3
5	1		2	9				

		2		9	8			4
6	9	4	2			8	3	1
7	1			3		5		
2	4	9	5		7			3
8		6		1	4			5
1	7	5		2			4	
			7				5	2
		7		5			1	
5	8	1	6	4		3		7

2	8	9	5		6		4	1
		5		8		9	3	
3	1		7		2	8	5	
1		8	9	7				
			6	2			9	
9		6		4		3	2	8
6				1	4		8	
	9	2		5	7			
		1	2	6	9		7	5

3	4	1		6	9		7	
7	9	8			2			5
		2	3		7	4	1	
	8	6		1				3
4	3	5			8	7		1
1	7			2			8	6
			2	5		3		
6	2	4		3	1			7
				7	4	1		2

3	1	8		2				7
7					9			
9	2	5				1	8	4
2	9			5	3	7	4	
		7	1			9	6	
8	5		9			3		2
	8	2	3			5		
5	4					8	3	6
6					8	4		1

		6			8	2	5	3
			9		5		8	
5	4		3			1	9	
8	3	1						2
					2	9		1
				1	3		6	
4	8	7	2		6	3	1	
9		5		3	1	6	4	8
	6					7	2	5

	7	3		6			1	
		4	2		8		9	
	2	8	1		9	6		4
			8				5	
6	3		5				8	1
	5			1		2		9
3		5	9	4	2		7	
	1		7		3		4	
7	4		6	8		5	2	

6	4	3	9	7				2
7		8	5				1	9
	1	5	4		8	7	3	6
3		9		5	2	1	8	
5	8			1		6	2	
2	6	1		4	7	3	9	
1	5		7		4		6	
8			2		3	5		1
	3			9	5			

		1	5					4
8	7		4	2		5		
5		4	9			2		
2			1	5		3	8	7
7	4		8	3				
1	3			7			5	
6	8	3	7			9		2
	1		3			7		
9	5	7		6			4	3

6		2		8	5	1	9	3
8			9		6		2	
	5	9	4		2		8	
4	6		2		7		3	
		1	6		3			
			1	4	8	7	5	
2			8		1	3		5
	1	6		2		8	7	9
7			3		9	4	1	

9	3			1				5
1	2		4	6		9		
5	8	6		2	9		7	1
4	6	3		5	8		1	9
	5	1	6		2		4	3
2	7	9	1	3	4	8	5	6
6							8	
3				7	6	1		
7	1						6	

	9		6	1	3		8	
		6	7		4	9		
							7	
8			4			7	5	
2	4		1	5	7	3	6	8
6	7	5		3	9	4	2	
	3	8		6	2		4	5
1	5	4	3		8		9	
						8		7

	5	2		7		8	1	9
4	9	3		1	8			
8		7	5		9		2	4
	6			4		7	5	
		1	7			4		2
7		5		2	6	9	3	
			6			5		3
5	8		4	3	1	2	9	
3					7	1	4	

6	7		9	4	2			
9		4	8	7				
8	2			1	5			
	3	7				6		5
	5	9	7			1		
4	6		2					7
	9	1			4	7	8	
7			3	8	9	2	5	
	8		1			9	3	

1	7					2	6	
	2	4	9		6	5		8
				1		4	7	
8	9	2	6			1		7
	1			9		6	3	2
4		6	7	2	1			
	6	7	1	3				
							5	6
2	4		8	6		7	9	

3		2	4		9		7	
5	6				2	3	4	
	7		8	3	6	2		5
1		7		2		8		3
	3		5	9	8	7		
8	4	5	3	1	7	6	2	9
		4				9	3	2
7		3	9	6	5		8	1
	1			4	3			

	4	8	5	2			6	7
7	5		6	3	8			1
		3	4		9	2	8	
	2	9	3	1	4	8	7	6
		1	9		6	5	3	
3	8	6	7	5	2	4		
2					7		9	
8			1	4		6	2	
	1			9				8

	1	7	9	8		2	5	6
5	9	3	6		2		8	
		2	4		5	3		9
	7		8	4	6	5		
6			5	2	7	9	1	8
2	5	8	3			6		7
3				6			9	
9	2			3		8	6	
			2	5	9			1

4	5	9	1		2	8	7	
7	2	3		8	5			1
6	8	1	7	3		9		5
3			5	1		7	9	
8			4		9		1	6
1			6			5		8
2				5		1		
				4		6		7
5			3	9	7			4

2		8	7	5			4	
			9	3	1	2		
		1		4	8			6
6	2	9		1	7	4	5	3
	3			2	9		6	
1	7	4				8	9	2
	1		6		4			8
5		6		9				4
	4	3	5	8		6		9

							8	
9	2						4	6
6	1				9	5		3
	5		3	7			2	1
	3					4		
			6	1	2			8
	7	3		8	5	6	9	
	8	1	4		6	7		5
5	6	9			3	8	1	4

				1	5		8	
	6	8			3		7	
5	9	1	6	7		3	4	
	2		5		4	7	1	9
	7		3	8	1		2	5
	4		7	9	2	8	6	
2		4	1			6		
9	1	7	8	5	6	2		
	5		2	4	7			8

	7	1		5	4		3	6
		2	7	1	3	4		
4		5		2	9			8
1	6	3		8	2	7	5	
				4	1			
8	4		5		6	3	2	1
2		4	1				8	
3	1	8	2		5	6		
	5					9		2

	1	7		9	5	8	3	2
2	8	4	7		1	5	9	6
3			8	2	6	7	1	
	3	1		8	7	2		
	9	2		1	3			
	6	8		4	9	1	5	
9	7			6				
	2	6				9		
1		5	9			3	6	

	4	7		8		3		
	3	9		7		6	2	8
1						4		
4	1			6	9	8	7	
	7		3				4	6
	9	6	5		7	2	1	
7				9	6	1	3	4
		1			5			2
		4		2	1	5	8	

		7		3	4			
3		4		7		5		1
	8	5		9				
	7				3	1	4	8
	3		8	4			5	7
	2	8		1	5		3	9
8	5	9	3	6	7	4	1	2
	4	2	1	5		8	6	3
	6	3		8	2			

5	9	2		8			4	3
1			2	3				9
3	4	7			6			8
					8			
		3		6	2		1	
6	1		7	9	5	3		
		6	5	7	3		9	1
		1		4	9		7	5
9			8				3	

9					5	4		6
7	4	8	9	3	6			5
6	1	5			8			
	8		4	1			6	9
5		1		6				4
		6	5			2	1	3
8	6	4	7	5	1		9	2
2		7		9	3		4	1
	3		6	2	4			

3		8	2		6	5	7	9
9	4	5	7	1	8	3		
			9	5	3	8		1
8			3	9	2			
1	3	4	5	6		2		8
6	9	2						
5	2	3			1	9		6
4	6	9				1		
					9		5	3

9	8	2	3			7		
4		6	7		8	3	1	9
	3		9			2	8	6
8		4	1	7			2	3
1	6	3			5		9	
	7			9	3			1
6	1	7		4	2			5
	2	9		3		1		8
3		8		1				

				7		3		
	4	2	3	8		5		
5		3	1			8	4	9
3		4		9	8	1		
	9				1	4	7	
	1	6			4	9	2	
4		9	6	1	2	7	8	
6	8		9	5	7		3	
2	5	7	8			6	9	

3	4	6		5		2		
7		9				8		5
5	8		4	2	7			6
9		7	1	8	4	6	3	2
8				7	6		5	
			2	3	5			8
4	7				8	1		
		8		4		7		9
			7	1			8	

7	9	3		8	1	4		2
	2		6	7	3	5	8	
			9	2		1		7
	3	9			8	2		4
1	7		3		6	8		
5	8	4	2	1			7	3
	6		4		5	7	2	
		5	8	3	7	9		
9			1		2	3		

	1	3	5	9	4	7	2	
2	9	5			8		6	
4	7				1	3		
9				5		8		2
	5				2			
1	8	2	7		9			
7	2			1				3
5		1	2		3	4	7	
8	3	9				2	5	

2		3	7		1	6	8	
	7	4	2	8	5			1
5	8	1			3		4	7
		9		7		5	2	3
	6			1			7	
7				5	9	1		
4						8	5	9
	3	6		9	4	7	1	
9			1				3	6

4	1	8		3			9	5
5	7	3	1					8
	9		8					
		7				2	5	
	5	2	3	8	7	9		
	4	1	5		2			
			6	5	8	3	7	
3			7	1	4		6	2
		5	9		3	1		4

9			7	2	3		1	
		2	6		4			9
	5	4				7		
6	3	5	8	7	2	4	9	
8	9	7	4	6	1			5
	2	1	9	3	5	6		7
5				1				
		8	5		9		7	
		9	3			1		6

9	7	8	5		2	3	1	
3			9			5		6
	5			7	3	9	2	8
	4	3		1	5	6	9	7
			6	4				
	8	9	2			1	4	
8				9	1			2
	9	5	4	2			3	
		2				4		

	7	9			1		8	
2	4		9	8				
8		1	3	7	4	2	9	
5					2	6		
			5		6	1	3	9
6	1	4						5
	3				8		5	
4				3	9	8		1
9	2		1	5	7	4	6	

3	2	7	5			9		
4		9		8			5	
	6	8						
	7	5	3	1	8	4	9	
					6		7	
		2		5	7	6		
1	5		2	9				7
2	9		8	7	4			1
	8				5	2	3	9

3			4	6	5		2	1
			8		3			
4			1		7	6	8	
9	2	4	7				6	5
8	1		2			4	9	7
	6			4	8	3	1	2
	8	9				2		6
		5	6			1	4	8
6	4	1					5	9

		9	2	5	1	6		8
8	6	5		4			3	
			6	8	3	4	5	
	2		8	3			6	7
6	9	8	1	7				
	4		5		6	1		
9			4	1		7		
3	1				8	5		6
2	5		3		9		1	

		9		8	2	5	6	3
2		5						
6		4	5	1	7		9	2
5	4	3	7			9		
	6	8						7
	1		6			4	5	
	9			7			4	
		6	9	4	5		8	1
4	5			6		3		9

		8	2		9	6		7
2	1	6	4		7		5	
		3				2	4	1
8	3	5	9	7		4		6
7		4	8	6	1	5		3
	9					7	2	8
4		7		5	3	9	8	
3			6					5
1	5	2				3	6	4

4	8	3	1		9		7	5
1	2		3				6	
5	6			8	2	9		3
8		1		4				
		5	9	2		3		6
	9				8		4	
3		8	6					9
6			2		3	7	5	
	5					6	3	1

			9		8		7	4
1	9			3				
7	8	2	1		4		6	3
	7				2	6	5	1
	2	8	5	7			3	
4	5			9				
5		9	7					8
	1	7		8		3		6
		6	2			5	4	

	9		4			2	8	7
6			8		2	4		
4			7	1		6		5
		9	5	6	1		4	
7				9	8			1
	1	6		7				
9	4	2		8	7	3		6
	6		9				7	
	5	7	6			9		8

	8					1	4	5
4			7		1	2	3	
3				4				6
7		1	4	3	8			
8	2	3	1	6		9	7	4
	5	4		7	9			3
5	7	6		8		3	2	1
9			5			4	8	7
1					7	6	5	

	2	6		8				3
9			7		4			
3		5	1	2		8	7	9
5			8	6	7		3	
2	3	4	9		1	7		8
6		8	2	4		5		1
			3			6		
4			6	1				
					8	3	2	5

	1	8			4		3	5
		6	3	7		8		
2			8					
	6	2			8		9	
9		5			1	3		8
	8	4	2	3	9		6	
6		9	1	8	7			3
	4	1	5	9		6	7	2
5	3	7			6	9	8	1

3							8	4
	2	6	5	4		3		
	9	4	6	3			5	
		3		7		9		
		1		5		7		
2	8	7	9	6	3	5		1
4	5				6	8	3	
7	3			9				6
6			3		2			5

9		5			6		7	
3		2		5		6	9	8
	7	8			2	1		
		6		9			8	
8		3	6			7		2
	5	1	2	7	8		6	3
1	8	7	3					6
	6				5	3	1	7
	3	4	1	6				9

8	9		2		6		4	1
		6	4	1				7
4			3	9		2	6	8
9	1				7		3	
	3	2	9		4	8	1	5
6		4	8	3	1	7		2
5		9	7				2	4
1	8	3			2	5	7	
		7	1			6		

	2	4		5	1		3	7
5				9		1		8
		1		2	7	4	9	5
	1		9	4	3	8		6
7	8	9	5		2	3		1
	4					2	5	9
4	9			3				2
1	3		2		9	5		4
				7		9		3

4		7	2	3				5
2		5		8	6			1
		6	4	5		3		
7			6	9	5		3	
	4	8			3			6
	5				4	9	1	
3	8	4		1	9	2	6	
		2		4	8	1		3
				6	2		4	

7	1	3		8				5
		4	3	5	1			
9	8	5		2	6		1	
3		7	6	1		2		4
	4				9			
6		1		3	5	9		
8	7	9		6				
		6		4	2		7	9
	5	2	8	9		1		

7	6	2			1	8	5	
	9	1		2	5	7	6	3
	5	8		6			1	2
		6	9	7	4			8
	4		6			9	7	
9		7				6		4
	1							5
5			2	3		1		6
		4	1		6			

			1	3	5	4	2	
		6	9					
5	4	1			2	8	9	3
4		8	2	9	3	6	1	
		2		4	1			
1		3	5					4
8	1		3	2			6	
		7		5		1	4	2
9		5	4	1	6		8	

8		4	3	7	9		1	
	3		5		1	6		
	2			4	8			
4			1		6	2	9	7
6		7						3
3	1	2				8	5	6
1					2	9	7	
9	4	6				3	2	
					3		6	8

2		3	8		9	4		7
	1			6	2	8	9	5
8		6		4	5	2	3	1
	6		4				8	3
7					1		5	
1		8		5		9		
	4			3			2	8
	8	5		7	4	3	1	9
	7		1	9			4	6

5	3	7		8	4			
8	2	6		5	9			1
4				2	7	8	3	
	1	9			2		7	8
	4							
		8	5			4	9	2
	8	4				3		
1	5			4		2	8	7
6	7				5		1	4

2		6	5	8	3			
8	3	1	2					6
	7		1	4		3	8	
	1	7		6		2	3	
3	5			1		6		
		8			2	5		1
	9	4		3	8		2	5
6	8				1	7		3
					7			9

3	2			1	4	6		
	8			6				
4	6	1	8			9	5	
1					2	3	8	
5	3	2	4	8	1	7	9	6
8		4	3	9	6		2	
6			1	7	8	2	4	
			5	4	9	8	6	3
			6	2	3		1	

	8		1		5			
	5	1	6	9		4		
	9	6	4	7			5	
4	2				7		3	6
1		7	9	6		8		5
9	6	5	3			7	1	
	1		7		9			
6		9	8	3	1			
8			2		6	1	9	4

5		6	4			7		2
				5			3	6
2	8		7		1	5	4	9
1	3	5		4	6	2		7
9	4							5
	2			9	3			
8		9	3		5	1		4
			6	1		9		
	1	4		8	9	6		3

Solutions

Soluciones

Respostas

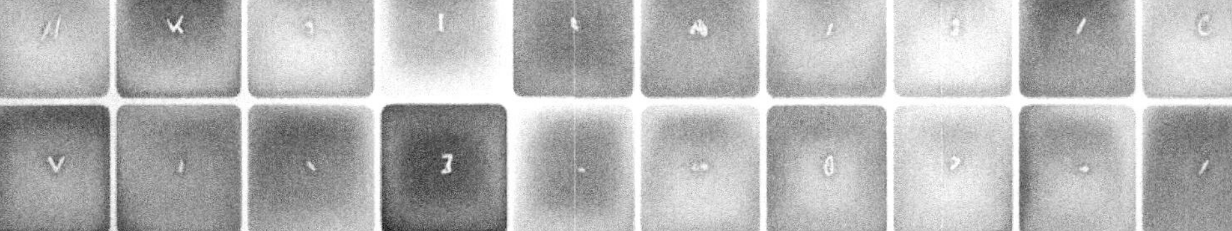

3	2	5	1	6	9	4	8	7
6	9	4	7	2	8	3	5	1
1	7	8	3	4	5	2	9	6
2	8	6	9	7	4	1	3	5
9	5	1	6	8	3	7	4	2
7	4	3	5	1	2	9	6	8
5	6	7	4	3	1	8	2	9
4	1	2	8	9	6	5	7	3
8	3	9	2	5	7	6	1	4

1	9	6	2	7	5	8	3	4
5	8	2	6	3	4	7	1	9
7	4	3	8	1	9	6	5	2
8	2	1	7	4	3	5	9	6
6	3	4	5	9	8	2	7	1
9	5	7	1	6	2	3	4	8
2	1	8	4	5	7	9	6	3
3	6	5	9	8	1	4	2	7
4	7	9	3	2	6	1	8	5

6	8	9	7	2	3	5	1	4
5	1	7	4	6	9	8	3	2
4	3	2	1	8	5	7	9	6
9	5	4	8	1	6	3	2	7
1	7	6	3	4	2	9	8	5
3	2	8	9	5	7	4	6	1
8	4	3	2	7	1	6	5	9
7	6	1	5	9	8	2	4	3
2	9	5	6	3	4	1	7	8

8	2	9	3	5	6	7	4	1
5	4	6	7	1	8	2	9	3
1	3	7	2	9	4	8	5	6
6	8	1	9	7	3	5	2	4
2	9	5	8	4	1	6	3	7
3	7	4	5	6	2	1	8	9
4	6	3	1	8	5	9	7	2
9	1	8	4	2	7	3	6	5
7	5	2	6	3	9	4	1	8

7	1	5	3	2	8	4	6	9
2	8	6	9	4	5	3	7	1
3	4	9	1	7	6	8	5	2
9	6	7	8	1	4	2	3	5
8	3	1	2	5	7	9	4	6
4	5	2	6	9	3	7	1	8
1	9	3	7	6	2	5	8	4
5	2	8	4	3	1	6	9	7
6	7	4	5	8	9	1	2	3

7	5	2	1	4	3	9	8	6
8	1	3	6	7	9	2	5	4
6	4	9	8	2	5	7	3	1
2	6	4	9	8	7	5	1	3
5	3	8	4	1	2	6	9	7
1	9	7	5	3	6	4	2	8
9	7	1	3	5	4	8	6	2
3	2	6	7	9	8	1	4	5
4	8	5	2	6	1	3	7	9

5	6	4	9	3	2	8	7	1
3	7	9	8	4	1	5	6	2
1	2	8	5	7	6	4	3	9
8	3	7	4	6	9	1	2	5
9	4	6	1	2	5	3	8	7
2	1	5	7	8	3	6	9	4
4	5	3	6	9	7	2	1	8
6	9	1	2	5	8	7	4	3
7	8	2	3	1	4	9	5	6

1	5	2	6	8	3	4	9	7
9	4	6	7	1	5	3	8	2
7	3	8	2	9	4	5	1	6
3	7	1	9	4	2	8	6	5
2	6	4	5	3	8	1	7	9
8	9	5	1	6	7	2	3	4
6	1	3	4	5	9	7	2	8
4	8	7	3	2	6	9	5	1
5	2	9	8	7	1	6	4	3

6	3	1	4	9	7	5	8	2
2	4	5	3	1	8	9	6	7
8	7	9	2	6	5	4	3	1
5	1	3	9	4	6	2	7	8
4	8	7	5	3	2	6	1	9
9	2	6	8	7	1	3	4	5
1	6	4	7	2	9	8	5	3
7	9	8	6	5	3	1	2	4
3	5	2	1	8	4	7	9	6

9	6	7	1	3	4	2	8	5
1	3	4	8	2	5	6	9	7
5	2	8	9	6	7	3	4	1
6	8	5	4	9	3	7	1	2
2	4	3	5	7	1	9	6	8
7	1	9	6	8	2	4	5	3
8	7	6	2	1	9	5	3	4
4	9	2	3	5	8	1	7	6
3	5	1	7	4	6	8	2	9

2	3	5	9	8	4	1	7	6
1	7	6	5	3	2	4	8	9
9	4	8	6	7	1	2	3	5
8	1	3	4	5	7	9	6	2
7	6	4	1	2	9	3	5	8
5	9	2	3	6	8	7	4	1
3	2	1	8	4	6	5	9	7
6	5	9	7	1	3	8	2	4
4	8	7	2	9	5	6	1	3

4	9	2	3	7	6	5	1	8
8	3	6	2	1	5	7	4	9
7	1	5	9	8	4	2	3	6
6	7	3	8	4	9	1	5	2
1	5	4	7	6	2	9	8	3
9	2	8	5	3	1	4	6	7
3	8	9	4	5	7	6	2	1
5	6	7	1	2	3	8	9	4
2	4	1	6	9	8	3	7	5

1	7	6	8	5	9	4	3	2
8	3	4	2	1	7	6	5	9
9	2	5	6	4	3	1	7	8
2	4	8	3	7	6	9	1	5
6	1	7	4	9	5	8	2	3
3	5	9	1	8	2	7	6	4
5	6	1	9	2	8	3	4	7
4	8	2	7	3	1	5	9	6
7	9	3	5	6	4	2	8	1

6	8	2	5	9	3	1	7	4
1	5	3	8	4	7	6	9	2
7	4	9	2	1	6	5	8	3
4	3	5	6	7	8	9	2	1
9	1	6	4	3	2	8	5	7
8	2	7	1	5	9	3	4	6
3	6	4	9	2	5	7	1	8
2	9	8	7	6	1	4	3	5
5	7	1	3	8	4	2	6	9

1	8	6	7	4	5	2	3	9
3	4	7	6	9	2	8	5	1
9	2	5	1	3	8	7	4	6
8	3	2	5	7	1	6	9	4
7	6	1	4	2	9	5	8	3
4	5	9	3	8	6	1	7	2
5	7	4	2	6	3	9	1	8
2	1	8	9	5	4	3	6	7
6	9	3	8	1	7	4	2	5

5	1	7	6	4	8	9	2	3
2	6	9	1	3	5	8	4	7
3	8	4	2	7	9	5	1	6
7	2	8	4	6	1	3	9	5
6	3	5	9	2	7	1	8	4
9	4	1	8	5	3	6	7	2
8	5	6	7	9	2	4	3	1
4	9	2	3	1	6	7	5	8
1	7	3	5	8	4	2	6	9

5	1	2	3	4	9	6	7	8
9	7	8	2	5	6	1	3	4
3	6	4	7	8	1	9	2	5
1	4	3	8	2	5	7	9	6
2	9	7	1	6	4	8	5	3
6	8	5	9	7	3	4	1	2
8	3	6	5	9	7	2	4	1
4	5	9	6	1	2	3	8	7
7	2	1	4	3	8	5	6	9

5	9	7	8	3	4	1	2	6
2	8	1	7	6	5	9	3	4
6	3	4	2	1	9	8	7	5
1	7	8	3	9	6	5	4	2
4	6	2	5	7	8	3	9	1
3	5	9	1	4	2	6	8	7
9	1	3	6	2	7	4	5	8
8	2	6	4	5	3	7	1	9
7	4	5	9	8	1	2	6	3

6	1	7	8	9	4	2	3	5
4	5	9	6	3	2	1	7	8
3	2	8	5	7	1	4	9	6
1	4	2	3	5	6	9	8	7
5	7	6	1	8	9	3	4	2
9	8	3	2	4	7	5	6	1
2	9	5	4	6	8	7	1	3
7	6	1	9	2	3	8	5	4
8	3	4	7	1	5	6	2	9

1	2	3	5	6	4	7	8	9
4	7	9	2	1	8	3	5	6
5	8	6	9	3	7	1	4	2
8	9	4	1	2	3	6	7	5
3	6	1	8	7	5	9	2	4
2	5	7	4	9	6	8	1	3
6	3	5	7	8	2	4	9	1
7	1	2	3	4	9	5	6	8
9	4	8	6	5	1	2	3	7

5	4	7	9	6	3	1	8	2
3	9	6	8	1	2	5	4	7
1	8	2	4	7	5	9	6	3
4	6	9	3	2	1	7	5	8
2	3	1	7	5	8	6	9	4
8	7	5	6	4	9	2	3	1
7	1	3	5	9	4	8	2	6
9	2	4	1	8	6	3	7	5
6	5	8	2	3	7	4	1	9

9	4	1	6	5	7	3	8	2
7	2	8	9	3	1	4	5	6
6	5	3	4	2	8	1	7	9
3	8	4	2	1	6	7	9	5
5	7	9	3	8	4	2	6	1
2	1	6	7	9	5	8	4	3
4	9	7	1	6	3	5	2	8
8	3	2	5	4	9	6	1	7
1	6	5	8	7	2	9	3	4

2	4	8	6	3	1	9	7	5
9	6	7	5	4	8	3	1	2
1	3	5	7	2	9	8	4	6
6	9	1	3	5	2	7	8	4
4	7	2	8	9	6	5	3	1
5	8	3	1	7	4	6	2	9
8	1	9	2	6	3	4	5	7
7	2	4	9	8	5	1	6	3
3	5	6	4	1	7	2	9	8

5	1	2	7	6	3	9	8	4
4	6	8	1	2	9	7	5	3
9	3	7	5	4	8	6	1	2
8	2	5	6	1	7	3	4	9
3	9	4	8	5	2	1	6	7
6	7	1	9	3	4	5	2	8
1	4	9	3	8	5	2	7	6
2	5	3	4	7	6	8	9	1
7	8	6	2	9	1	4	3	5

7	6	3	5	4	2	8	9	1
2	8	5	6	9	1	3	4	7
9	4	1	3	7	8	2	5	6
6	3	9	1	5	4	7	2	8
4	1	8	2	6	7	5	3	9
5	7	2	8	3	9	1	6	4
8	5	7	9	2	6	4	1	3
1	2	6	4	8	3	9	7	5
3	9	4	7	1	5	6	8	2

7	4	8	3	6	2	1	9	5
9	1	6	4	8	5	3	7	2
2	3	5	1	9	7	6	8	4
5	2	3	8	4	6	7	1	9
8	6	1	7	5	9	2	4	3
4	7	9	2	1	3	5	6	8
3	9	2	6	7	4	8	5	1
6	8	4	5	3	1	9	2	7
1	5	7	9	2	8	4	3	6

8	1	2	6	9	7	3	5	4
6	4	5	1	3	8	7	9	2
3	9	7	4	2	5	6	8	1
1	3	9	8	7	2	5	4	6
7	2	8	5	6	4	1	3	9
5	6	4	9	1	3	8	2	7
4	7	3	2	8	1	9	6	5
2	8	6	7	5	9	4	1	3
9	5	1	3	4	6	2	7	8

3	7	1	6	4	5	2	9	8
4	2	5	7	9	8	1	6	3
8	6	9	1	3	2	5	7	4
6	1	8	3	2	7	4	5	9
2	4	3	9	5	6	8	1	7
5	9	7	8	1	4	3	2	6
9	5	4	2	6	3	7	8	1
7	3	6	5	8	1	9	4	2
1	8	2	4	7	9	6	3	5

5	9	7	3	4	2	8	1	6
1	6	3	5	8	7	2	9	4
4	2	8	6	9	1	5	3	7
7	3	1	9	2	8	6	4	5
2	4	5	7	3	6	9	8	1
6	8	9	4	1	5	7	2	3
9	5	2	1	6	4	3	7	8
3	7	4	8	5	9	1	6	2
8	1	6	2	7	3	4	5	9

4	9	3	2	8	5	7	1	6
2	8	7	9	6	1	3	5	4
6	5	1	7	4	3	9	8	2
1	4	6	3	7	8	5	2	9
7	3	8	5	9	2	4	6	1
9	2	5	4	1	6	8	7	3
8	6	4	1	5	9	2	3	7
5	7	2	6	3	4	1	9	8
3	1	9	8	2	7	6	4	5

7	2	4	9	8	1	5	6	3
5	6	3	2	7	4	8	1	9
1	9	8	6	3	5	7	2	4
4	5	2	3	6	8	1	9	7
8	1	9	4	2	7	3	5	6
3	7	6	1	5	9	2	4	8
9	4	7	5	1	3	6	8	2
2	8	5	7	4	6	9	3	1
6	3	1	8	9	2	4	7	5

1	9	8	3	6	2	5	7	4
3	6	4	5	1	7	9	8	2
7	5	2	8	4	9	1	6	3
6	2	7	4	8	1	3	5	9
4	3	9	7	5	6	8	2	1
8	1	5	2	9	3	7	4	6
2	7	1	6	3	8	4	9	5
9	4	6	1	7	5	2	3	8
5	8	3	9	2	4	6	1	7

6	2	9	4	5	8	7	3	1
4	8	1	9	7	3	6	5	2
3	5	7	2	6	1	8	4	9
7	4	3	8	1	2	5	9	6
8	1	2	5	9	6	4	7	3
5	9	6	3	4	7	1	2	8
9	3	5	1	8	4	2	6	7
2	6	8	7	3	5	9	1	4
1	7	4	6	2	9	3	8	5

3	9	4	1	6	7	2	5	8
8	7	2	9	3	5	6	1	4
1	5	6	2	4	8	7	9	3
9	6	7	3	8	2	5	4	1
2	4	8	7	5	1	9	3	6
5	1	3	4	9	6	8	7	2
7	8	5	6	1	4	3	2	9
6	3	1	5	2	9	4	8	7
4	2	9	8	7	3	1	6	5

4	3	5	6	1	8	9	2	7
2	6	7	5	9	4	8	1	3
8	9	1	3	7	2	4	5	6
1	7	4	8	3	6	2	9	5
5	2	3	1	4	9	6	7	8
6	8	9	7	2	5	1	3	4
7	1	2	4	6	3	5	8	9
3	4	8	9	5	1	7	6	2
9	5	6	2	8	7	3	4	1

8	3	7	5	2	4	1	6	9
6	2	9	3	1	7	5	8	4
4	5	1	6	9	8	3	7	2
3	4	6	9	5	2	7	1	8
1	9	2	8	7	6	4	3	5
5	7	8	1	4	3	2	9	6
9	1	4	7	6	5	8	2	3
7	8	5	2	3	9	6	4	1
2	6	3	4	8	1	9	5	7

6	9	5	8	7	4	2	3	1
4	1	7	9	2	3	5	8	6
8	3	2	5	6	1	4	9	7
9	5	8	2	3	7	1	6	4
2	7	4	1	8	6	9	5	3
1	6	3	4	5	9	8	7	2
7	2	9	6	4	8	3	1	5
3	4	1	7	9	5	6	2	8
5	8	6	3	1	2	7	4	9

3	1	5	4	7	6	9	2	8
2	9	4	1	8	5	7	3	6
8	6	7	9	3	2	5	1	4
6	5	1	2	4	9	3	8	7
4	8	2	7	1	3	6	5	9
7	3	9	5	6	8	1	4	2
5	7	6	3	2	4	8	9	1
1	4	3	8	9	7	2	6	5
9	2	8	6	5	1	4	7	3

3	5	7	2	9	6	1	8	4
4	2	9	5	1	8	3	7	6
8	6	1	3	4	7	5	2	9
5	1	4	7	2	9	8	6	3
7	9	2	6	8	3	4	5	1
6	8	3	4	5	1	7	9	2
1	3	8	9	7	2	6	4	5
9	7	5	1	6	4	2	3	8
2	4	6	8	3	5	9	1	7

4	6	8	1	5	9	7	2	3
7	2	9	4	3	6	8	1	5
3	1	5	7	2	8	4	6	9
1	3	6	5	7	4	2	9	8
9	4	7	2	8	1	3	5	6
5	8	2	9	6	3	1	4	7
8	9	3	6	1	2	5	7	4
2	7	4	3	9	5	6	8	1
6	5	1	8	4	7	9	3	2

1	9	5	7	3	6	8	2	4
2	8	6	5	1	4	9	7	3
4	3	7	8	9	2	6	1	5
7	1	8	2	4	3	5	9	6
5	4	2	9	6	8	7	3	1
9	6	3	1	7	5	2	4	8
3	5	9	4	8	7	1	6	2
8	7	4	6	2	1	3	5	9
6	2	1	3	5	9	4	8	7

3	2	1	6	7	9	4	8	5
9	6	5	1	8	4	2	3	7
4	8	7	2	3	5	9	6	1
2	7	3	8	5	6	1	9	4
5	1	9	4	2	3	8	7	6
6	4	8	7	9	1	3	5	2
7	3	6	9	1	2	5	4	8
1	5	4	3	6	8	7	2	9
8	9	2	5	4	7	6	1	3

3	5	9	7	4	2	8	1	6
1	2	8	6	3	5	4	9	7
7	6	4	8	9	1	2	5	3
6	9	3	1	7	4	5	2	8
4	7	1	2	5	8	3	6	9
5	8	2	9	6	3	7	4	1
2	3	6	5	1	7	9	8	4
8	1	7	4	2	9	6	3	5
9	4	5	3	8	6	1	7	2

9	1	4	2	8	3	7	5	6
3	8	5	1	6	7	4	9	2
2	7	6	9	4	5	8	1	3
5	3	7	4	2	6	9	8	1
4	2	9	7	1	8	6	3	5
1	6	8	5	3	9	2	4	7
8	9	2	6	5	1	3	7	4
6	5	3	8	7	4	1	2	9
7	4	1	3	9	2	5	6	8

5	6	2	4	3	1	8	9	7
7	8	9	5	2	6	4	1	3
3	1	4	7	8	9	6	2	5
9	3	8	6	7	4	1	5	2
6	7	1	3	5	2	9	8	4
4	2	5	9	1	8	7	3	6
8	5	6	2	9	7	3	4	1
2	9	7	1	4	3	5	6	8
1	4	3	8	6	5	2	7	9

8	6	7	9	4	3	2	1	5
4	3	9	2	1	5	6	8	7
2	1	5	8	6	7	3	9	4
1	8	3	7	5	9	4	2	6
6	9	4	3	2	1	5	7	8
7	5	2	6	8	4	1	3	9
9	7	1	4	3	6	8	5	2
5	4	8	1	7	2	9	6	3
3	2	6	5	9	8	7	4	1

6	3	4	1	7	2	9	5	8
8	1	2	6	5	9	3	7	4
9	7	5	4	3	8	2	6	1
3	5	6	9	8	7	1	4	2
2	9	7	3	1	4	5	8	6
4	8	1	2	6	5	7	3	9
5	6	3	8	2	1	4	9	7
1	4	8	7	9	3	6	2	5
7	2	9	5	4	6	8	1	3

1	6	7	9	2	8	3	5	4
4	3	2	7	6	5	8	9	1
9	8	5	1	4	3	7	6	2
2	4	8	5	3	7	9	1	6
5	1	9	6	8	4	2	7	3
3	7	6	2	1	9	5	4	8
6	5	3	4	9	2	1	8	7
7	2	4	8	5	1	6	3	9
8	9	1	3	7	6	4	2	5

3	9	1	6	7	5	2	4	8
8	6	2	4	3	1	7	9	5
5	4	7	2	9	8	1	3	6
6	2	9	1	8	7	3	5	4
7	3	8	5	4	9	6	1	2
1	5	4	3	6	2	9	8	7
9	1	6	7	5	4	8	2	3
4	8	3	9	2	6	5	7	1
2	7	5	8	1	3	4	6	9

8	9	2	6	1	7	4	5	3
5	4	1	8	2	3	6	9	7
3	6	7	4	9	5	8	1	2
9	5	8	3	6	1	7	2	4
1	3	6	2	7	4	9	8	5
2	7	4	5	8	9	3	6	1
6	8	3	1	4	2	5	7	9
7	1	5	9	3	8	2	4	6
4	2	9	7	5	6	1	3	8

2	3	5	7	4	1	9	6	8
1	8	6	9	5	2	4	7	3
7	4	9	3	6	8	1	2	5
9	2	8	4	7	3	6	5	1
3	1	7	5	8	6	2	4	9
5	6	4	1	2	9	3	8	7
4	9	2	8	1	7	5	3	6
6	7	3	2	9	5	8	1	4
8	5	1	6	3	4	7	9	2

7	3	5	2	6	4	8	1	9
1	6	9	8	3	7	5	4	2
2	4	8	1	9	5	6	3	7
9	8	4	6	5	1	2	7	3
5	7	3	4	2	8	9	6	1
6	2	1	3	7	9	4	8	5
8	9	7	5	1	6	3	2	4
4	5	2	7	8	3	1	9	6
3	1	6	9	4	2	7	5	8

5	9	1	8	3	4	2	6	7
3	8	2	6	9	7	5	4	1
4	7	6	1	2	5	3	9	8
2	1	3	9	8	6	4	7	5
9	4	8	5	7	2	6	1	3
7	6	5	4	1	3	8	2	9
1	2	4	7	5	8	9	3	6
6	5	7	3	4	9	1	8	2
8	3	9	2	6	1	7	5	4

8	2	7	9	6	5	4	3	1
4	9	3	1	2	7	5	6	8
6	1	5	4	3	8	2	9	7
3	5	1	2	8	4	9	7	6
7	8	4	5	9	6	3	1	2
2	6	9	7	1	3	8	5	4
9	7	2	8	5	1	6	4	3
5	4	6	3	7	2	1	8	9
1	3	8	6	4	9	7	2	5

7	8	3	9	1	6	2	5	4
1	5	6	3	2	4	7	8	9
2	4	9	8	5	7	6	1	3
8	6	1	5	4	2	9	3	7
5	7	2	6	9	3	1	4	8
9	3	4	7	8	1	5	2	6
4	2	8	1	7	9	3	6	5
6	9	5	2	3	8	4	7	1
3	1	7	4	6	5	8	9	2

8	1	4	9	6	2	5	3	7
7	9	2	3	4	5	8	1	6
5	6	3	7	1	8	4	9	2
2	3	8	4	7	9	1	6	5
6	7	5	8	3	1	9	2	4
9	4	1	5	2	6	3	7	8
4	2	9	1	8	7	6	5	3
3	5	7	6	9	4	2	8	1
1	8	6	2	5	3	7	4	9

8	2	7	4	9	1	5	6	3
4	9	3	6	8	5	2	7	1
5	1	6	7	3	2	4	8	9
7	5	8	3	2	4	9	1	6
9	3	4	8	1	6	7	5	2
1	6	2	5	7	9	3	4	8
6	4	9	1	5	3	8	2	7
2	8	5	9	6	7	1	3	4
3	7	1	2	4	8	6	9	5

2	3	6	7	9	8	4	5	1
9	5	4	6	3	1	2	7	8
1	7	8	5	2	4	3	6	9
6	4	7	8	5	2	9	1	3
8	1	3	9	6	7	5	4	2
5	9	2	4	1	3	6	8	7
4	2	5	1	8	9	7	3	6
3	6	1	2	7	5	8	9	4
7	8	9	3	4	6	1	2	5

6	5	1	8	9	2	7	3	4
3	7	2	6	4	1	8	5	9
9	8	4	5	3	7	1	2	6
5	4	8	9	1	6	3	7	2
2	6	7	3	8	5	4	9	1
1	3	9	2	7	4	6	8	5
4	2	5	7	6	8	9	1	3
8	9	6	1	2	3	5	4	7
7	1	3	4	5	9	2	6	8

3	5	1	4	2	8	7	9	6
9	8	7	3	5	6	1	2	4
4	2	6	7	9	1	3	8	5
5	4	8	1	7	2	6	3	9
7	6	3	9	4	5	8	1	2
2	1	9	6	8	3	4	5	7
6	9	5	8	1	7	2	4	3
1	3	4	2	6	9	5	7	8
8	7	2	5	3	4	9	6	1

4	3	2	1	9	8	7	6	5
6	1	7	5	3	2	8	4	9
9	8	5	4	6	7	1	2	3
2	9	6	8	1	4	3	5	7
3	5	4	9	7	6	2	1	8
8	7	1	2	5	3	4	9	6
7	2	3	6	4	9	5	8	1
1	4	9	7	8	5	6	3	2
5	6	8	3	2	1	9	7	4

6	5	1	9	7	8	3	2	4
9	8	2	4	6	3	1	7	5
4	3	7	2	1	5	8	9	6
7	6	8	5	2	4	9	3	1
5	1	4	7	3	9	6	8	2
2	9	3	1	8	6	4	5	7
3	7	6	8	5	1	2	4	9
8	2	9	6	4	7	5	1	3
1	4	5	3	9	2	7	6	8

4	2	1	6	9	8	7	3	5
5	3	6	7	2	4	9	8	1
9	7	8	1	5	3	6	4	2
2	9	5	4	1	6	8	7	3
3	1	4	2	8	7	5	9	6
8	6	7	9	3	5	1	2	4
6	4	3	8	7	1	2	5	9
7	5	2	3	6	9	4	1	8
1	8	9	5	4	2	3	6	7

4	3	9	8	6	1	2	5	7
6	5	2	9	4	7	3	1	8
8	1	7	2	3	5	6	9	4
7	6	3	5	2	9	4	8	1
1	2	5	4	7	8	9	3	6
9	4	8	3	1	6	7	2	5
2	7	1	6	8	3	5	4	9
5	8	4	7	9	2	1	6	3
3	9	6	1	5	4	8	7	2

8	1	9	5	2	7	4	3	6
6	7	4	3	1	8	9	2	5
3	5	2	6	9	4	1	7	8
1	4	7	9	6	2	5	8	3
2	6	8	4	5	3	7	9	1
5	9	3	8	7	1	6	4	2
4	3	6	1	8	9	2	5	7
9	2	1	7	3	5	8	6	4
7	8	5	2	4	6	3	1	9

3	5	2	8	7	1	9	6	4
1	4	7	6	3	9	5	8	2
9	8	6	4	2	5	1	7	3
7	9	4	1	6	3	2	5	8
2	6	3	7	5	8	4	9	1
8	1	5	9	4	2	7	3	6
6	3	9	5	1	4	8	2	7
5	7	1	2	8	6	3	4	9
4	2	8	3	9	7	6	1	5

6	1	5	2	7	9	4	8	3
4	9	8	3	1	5	7	6	2
3	2	7	4	6	8	5	9	1
5	8	2	7	4	6	3	1	9
9	3	4	5	2	1	8	7	6
1	7	6	9	8	3	2	5	4
8	6	3	1	5	2	9	4	7
2	4	1	8	9	7	6	3	5
7	5	9	6	3	4	1	2	8

3	4	9	5	6	2	8	1	7
6	1	8	3	9	7	4	5	2
2	7	5	8	1	4	9	3	6
1	3	4	6	8	9	7	2	5
9	2	7	4	5	3	6	8	1
5	8	6	2	7	1	3	9	4
4	9	3	7	2	5	1	6	8
8	5	1	9	4	6	2	7	3
7	6	2	1	3	8	5	4	9

4	3	8	2	9	5	6	7	1
5	1	9	6	7	4	2	3	8
2	7	6	8	1	3	4	9	5
6	9	2	1	8	7	3	5	4
7	4	1	3	5	6	9	8	2
8	5	3	9	4	2	1	6	7
3	6	4	7	2	8	5	1	9
1	2	7	5	6	9	8	4	3
9	8	5	4	3	1	7	2	6

8	7	5	2	1	6	3	9	4
2	9	4	5	3	7	1	6	8
1	3	6	9	8	4	7	5	2
7	6	1	8	4	3	9	2	5
5	2	3	7	6	9	4	8	1
9	4	8	1	5	2	6	7	3
4	1	7	6	2	5	8	3	9
6	8	2	3	9	1	5	4	7
3	5	9	4	7	8	2	1	6

1	6	7	5	4	2	8	3	9
3	5	2	6	9	8	4	7	1
8	9	4	7	1	3	2	5	6
6	8	5	2	7	1	3	9	4
7	4	9	3	6	5	1	8	2
2	3	1	4	8	9	7	6	5
4	7	3	9	2	6	5	1	8
5	1	6	8	3	4	9	2	7
9	2	8	1	5	7	6	4	3

4	8	2	1	3	6	5	7	9
7	1	9	5	2	8	3	6	4
3	6	5	7	4	9	2	8	1
9	5	3	8	7	1	4	2	6
6	4	1	9	5	2	7	3	8
2	7	8	3	6	4	1	9	5
1	2	6	4	8	7	9	5	3
5	9	7	6	1	3	8	4	2
8	3	4	2	9	5	6	1	7

3	8	9	6	5	1	4	7	2
2	6	5	8	7	4	3	9	1
4	7	1	3	2	9	8	6	5
5	2	7	1	8	6	9	3	4
9	1	4	5	3	7	6	2	8
8	3	6	4	9	2	1	5	7
1	5	8	7	6	3	2	4	9
7	9	3	2	4	8	5	1	6
6	4	2	9	1	5	7	8	3

5	6	7	9	1	4	8	2	3
3	9	8	6	7	2	4	5	1
4	1	2	8	5	3	6	7	9
1	3	5	2	4	7	9	8	6
7	2	9	3	8	6	5	1	4
6	8	4	1	9	5	2	3	7
8	7	3	5	6	9	1	4	2
9	4	1	7	2	8	3	6	5
2	5	6	4	3	1	7	9	8

8	5	7	4	6	3	1	9	2
4	3	1	9	8	2	7	5	6
2	6	9	7	1	5	3	8	4
9	1	8	2	3	6	5	4	7
7	2	6	5	9	4	8	3	1
3	4	5	1	7	8	6	2	9
5	7	3	6	4	9	2	1	8
1	8	4	3	2	7	9	6	5
6	9	2	8	5	1	4	7	3

9	7	8	1	6	2	3	4	5
5	3	4	8	9	7	2	6	1
6	2	1	4	3	5	7	9	8
8	9	5	7	2	4	6	1	3
7	6	2	3	8	1	4	5	9
4	1	3	9	5	6	8	2	7
2	4	9	5	7	8	1	3	6
3	8	6	2	1	9	5	7	4
1	5	7	6	4	3	9	8	2

3	8	5	7	9	2	6	4	1
9	2	4	1	8	6	3	7	5
7	1	6	5	4	3	2	9	8
2	9	1	6	5	4	8	3	7
8	5	7	9	3	1	4	6	2
4	6	3	2	7	8	5	1	9
6	3	9	8	2	7	1	5	4
5	4	2	3	1	9	7	8	6
1	7	8	4	6	5	9	2	3

1	3	8	5	4	6	2	7	9
6	2	7	1	9	8	3	5	4
9	4	5	7	3	2	1	8	6
4	1	2	9	6	5	8	3	7
5	9	6	3	8	7	4	2	1
7	8	3	4	2	1	6	9	5
3	7	9	2	1	4	5	6	8
2	6	4	8	5	9	7	1	3
8	5	1	6	7	3	9	4	2

1	3	2	7	8	6	4	9	5
9	5	4	2	3	1	8	6	7
6	7	8	4	5	9	3	1	2
5	4	9	8	2	7	1	3	6
2	1	7	3	6	4	5	8	9
8	6	3	1	9	5	7	2	4
7	2	6	5	1	8	9	4	3
4	9	1	6	7	3	2	5	8
3	8	5	9	4	2	6	7	1

4	7	2	3	1	9	6	5	8
3	1	6	5	7	8	2	9	4
5	8	9	4	2	6	3	1	7
2	6	7	1	9	3	8	4	5
1	4	5	2	8	7	9	6	3
9	3	8	6	4	5	1	7	2
8	5	1	9	3	4	7	2	6
6	2	3	7	5	1	4	8	9
7	9	4	8	6	2	5	3	1

4	2	5	7	3	9	1	6	8
6	9	8	2	4	1	5	7	3
3	7	1	6	8	5	2	4	9
7	4	3	5	6	2	8	9	1
5	6	2	9	1	8	4	3	7
8	1	9	4	7	3	6	2	5
9	5	7	1	2	4	3	8	6
1	3	4	8	9	6	7	5	2
2	8	6	3	5	7	9	1	4

7	1	5	6	4	3	9	2	8
9	3	8	5	2	7	4	1	6
6	2	4	8	1	9	3	7	5
5	4	2	3	8	6	1	9	7
1	7	9	2	5	4	8	6	3
3	8	6	7	9	1	2	5	4
8	5	3	1	6	2	7	4	9
4	6	1	9	7	8	5	3	2
2	9	7	4	3	5	6	8	1

3	1	4	8	2	5	7	9	6
8	6	5	7	4	9	1	2	3
2	9	7	6	1	3	8	5	4
9	2	3	5	7	4	6	8	1
6	4	8	9	3	1	2	7	5
5	7	1	2	8	6	3	4	9
7	3	9	4	6	2	5	1	8
4	8	6	1	5	7	9	3	2
1	5	2	3	9	8	4	6	7

5	9	2	3	1	8	4	7	6
3	1	4	5	7	6	2	8	9
8	6	7	4	2	9	5	3	1
7	4	8	6	5	2	9	1	3
9	3	1	7	8	4	6	2	5
2	5	6	1	9	3	8	4	7
4	7	3	2	6	5	1	9	8
1	8	5	9	4	7	3	6	2
6	2	9	8	3	1	7	5	4

7	4	3	6	5	2	8	9	1
6	9	2	3	1	8	4	7	5
1	5	8	7	9	4	6	3	2
5	6	7	1	4	3	9	2	8
8	2	4	9	7	5	3	1	6
3	1	9	8	2	6	7	5	4
2	7	5	4	8	9	1	6	3
4	3	1	5	6	7	2	8	9
9	8	6	2	3	1	5	4	7

5	2	9	1	6	8	7	3	4
8	6	7	3	9	4	5	2	1
3	1	4	5	2	7	6	9	8
7	9	3	8	5	1	2	4	6
2	8	5	6	4	9	1	7	3
1	4	6	2	7	3	8	5	9
4	3	8	7	1	2	9	6	5
9	5	2	4	8	6	3	1	7
6	7	1	9	3	5	4	8	2

2	8	3	7	9	4	5	6	1
6	1	5	2	3	8	4	9	7
9	4	7	5	6	1	3	2	8
1	7	4	9	8	5	6	3	2
3	5	2	6	1	7	9	8	4
8	6	9	3	4	2	7	1	5
4	3	8	1	5	9	2	7	6
7	9	1	4	2	6	8	5	3
5	2	6	8	7	3	1	4	9

6	2	4	3	1	8	5	7	9
9	3	7	4	6	5	2	8	1
5	1	8	9	2	7	6	4	3
1	9	3	6	8	4	7	5	2
8	7	5	2	9	1	3	6	4
4	6	2	7	5	3	1	9	8
2	8	6	1	7	9	4	3	5
3	5	1	8	4	6	9	2	7
7	4	9	5	3	2	8	1	6

1	6	5	4	3	7	9	2	8
4	7	2	1	8	9	5	6	3
8	9	3	2	5	6	7	4	1
5	1	7	3	6	2	4	8	9
3	2	4	5	9	8	6	1	7
9	8	6	7	4	1	3	5	2
7	5	8	9	2	4	1	3	6
6	4	1	8	7	3	2	9	5
2	3	9	6	1	5	8	7	4

1	9	7	5	4	8	3	6	2
4	2	5	1	6	3	8	7	9
8	3	6	2	9	7	4	5	1
2	8	3	9	5	1	6	4	7
9	7	4	8	2	6	5	1	3
5	6	1	3	7	4	2	9	8
6	1	9	4	3	2	7	8	5
3	4	8	7	1	5	9	2	6
7	5	2	6	8	9	1	3	4

3	5	8	6	1	2	7	9	4
4	2	9	8	7	5	6	3	1
6	7	1	4	3	9	2	8	5
2	9	3	5	4	6	1	7	8
5	8	4	7	2	1	3	6	9
1	6	7	3	9	8	4	5	2
9	4	5	1	6	7	8	2	3
7	3	2	9	8	4	5	1	6
8	1	6	2	5	3	9	4	7

3	7	2	9	6	1	8	4	5
6	9	8	4	5	3	2	7	1
4	5	1	2	8	7	6	9	3
1	6	9	7	2	8	3	5	4
8	2	4	3	1	5	7	6	9
7	3	5	6	9	4	1	8	2
2	8	7	1	4	9	5	3	6
9	1	3	5	7	6	4	2	8
5	4	6	8	3	2	9	1	7

6	7	8	9	5	1	2	3	4
2	5	1	6	4	3	8	7	9
9	4	3	2	8	7	1	6	5
5	6	4	3	7	8	9	2	1
7	3	9	1	2	4	6	5	8
1	8	2	5	6	9	7	4	3
8	1	7	4	3	2	5	9	6
3	9	6	7	1	5	4	8	2
4	2	5	8	9	6	3	1	7

2	7	5	3	8	6	1	9	4
8	1	6	9	2	4	3	7	5
3	9	4	1	5	7	8	6	2
5	2	9	6	3	1	4	8	7
4	8	1	7	9	5	6	2	3
6	3	7	8	4	2	5	1	9
1	6	3	4	7	9	2	5	8
7	4	2	5	6	8	9	3	1
9	5	8	2	1	3	7	4	6

7	8	6	3	1	2	4	9	5
4	1	2	7	5	9	6	3	8
3	5	9	4	6	8	1	7	2
2	3	7	9	4	5	8	1	6
8	9	1	6	2	3	7	5	4
6	4	5	1	8	7	9	2	3
9	2	8	5	7	6	3	4	1
1	6	3	2	9	4	5	8	7
5	7	4	8	3	1	2	6	9

1	8	7	4	9	6	3	5	2
2	6	9	3	8	5	7	1	4
5	3	4	1	2	7	9	6	8
8	4	5	9	1	2	6	3	7
7	2	6	8	5	3	4	9	1
9	1	3	7	6	4	2	8	5
4	5	1	6	7	9	8	2	3
6	7	8	2	3	1	5	4	9
3	9	2	5	4	8	1	7	6

4	3	6	5	2	1	9	8	7
9	1	2	8	7	4	5	3	6
5	7	8	9	3	6	2	1	4
7	9	3	1	4	5	6	2	8
8	2	4	7	6	3	1	9	5
1	6	5	2	8	9	4	7	3
2	8	9	4	5	7	3	6	1
6	5	7	3	1	2	8	4	9
3	4	1	6	9	8	7	5	2

3	9	8	1	6	7	5	2	4
2	4	1	9	5	8	6	3	7
7	5	6	3	4	2	1	8	9
1	6	3	5	8	4	9	7	2
5	2	9	6	7	3	4	1	8
8	7	4	2	1	9	3	6	5
6	8	5	4	2	1	7	9	3
4	3	2	7	9	6	8	5	1
9	1	7	8	3	5	2	4	6

8	5	2	7	3	6	1	9	4
7	9	4	1	2	5	3	6	8
3	1	6	8	4	9	7	5	2
2	6	1	9	8	3	5	4	7
5	4	8	2	6	7	9	1	3
9	7	3	5	1	4	8	2	6
6	3	5	4	9	8	2	7	1
1	8	9	6	7	2	4	3	5
4	2	7	3	5	1	6	8	9

8	9	3	6	7	4	5	1	2
5	7	4	2	1	9	8	3	6
1	2	6	8	5	3	9	4	7
3	5	8	4	9	2	6	7	1
7	6	9	3	8	1	4	2	5
4	1	2	5	6	7	3	8	9
2	4	5	1	3	6	7	9	8
6	3	7	9	2	8	1	5	4
9	8	1	7	4	5	2	6	3

2	5	4	6	7	1	8	9	3
1	7	9	4	3	8	2	5	6
8	3	6	5	2	9	7	4	1
9	8	2	7	6	4	1	3	5
7	6	3	2	1	5	4	8	9
4	1	5	8	9	3	6	2	7
6	2	8	3	5	7	9	1	4
5	9	7	1	4	2	3	6	8
3	4	1	9	8	6	5	7	2

5	6	2	1	4	8	3	7	9
8	1	3	7	5	9	2	4	6
9	4	7	6	2	3	5	1	8
6	3	4	8	1	2	9	5	7
1	7	9	3	6	5	8	2	4
2	5	8	9	7	4	6	3	1
3	2	6	4	8	7	1	9	5
4	8	5	2	9	1	7	6	3
7	9	1	5	3	6	4	8	2

2	3	4	6	9	7	5	8	1
9	1	8	4	2	5	6	3	7
5	6	7	1	8	3	4	9	2
1	8	9	7	5	2	3	6	4
6	2	5	9	3	4	7	1	8
7	4	3	8	1	6	2	5	9
4	7	1	5	6	8	9	2	3
3	9	6	2	7	1	8	4	5
8	5	2	3	4	9	1	7	6

1	8	9	4	7	5	3	6	2
6	4	5	2	8	3	1	7	9
3	2	7	6	9	1	4	8	5
8	5	2	1	6	4	7	9	3
9	1	3	5	2	7	6	4	8
7	6	4	8	3	9	5	2	1
5	9	8	3	4	6	2	1	7
2	3	6	7	1	8	9	5	4
4	7	1	9	5	2	8	3	6

2	4	8	3	7	5	6	9	1
7	1	5	9	2	6	3	8	4
6	9	3	8	1	4	2	5	7
3	2	9	6	8	7	4	1	5
8	6	7	5	4	1	9	3	2
4	5	1	2	9	3	8	7	6
9	7	4	1	3	2	5	6	8
5	8	2	7	6	9	1	4	3
1	3	6	4	5	8	7	2	9

7	9	8	1	4	5	6	3	2
4	2	1	7	3	6	8	9	5
6	3	5	9	8	2	7	1	4
1	5	9	8	6	7	2	4	3
8	7	3	4	2	1	5	6	9
2	4	6	5	9	3	1	7	8
3	1	4	2	7	8	9	5	6
9	8	7	6	5	4	3	2	1
5	6	2	3	1	9	4	8	7

5	1	6	2	8	9	7	4	3
2	4	9	5	3	7	6	8	1
8	7	3	6	4	1	2	9	5
3	8	7	9	1	6	4	5	2
6	9	2	7	5	4	1	3	8
4	5	1	3	2	8	9	6	7
9	3	4	8	7	2	5	1	6
1	2	8	4	6	5	3	7	9
7	6	5	1	9	3	8	2	4

1	9	7	4	3	8	2	6	5
8	3	4	2	6	5	1	9	7
5	6	2	7	9	1	4	8	3
6	5	9	8	1	7	3	4	2
3	7	1	6	2	4	8	5	9
4	2	8	3	5	9	7	1	6
2	4	3	5	8	6	9	7	1
7	1	5	9	4	3	6	2	8
9	8	6	1	7	2	5	3	4

8	4	7	5	1	3	6	2	9
9	5	6	2	4	7	8	1	3
1	2	3	6	9	8	4	5	7
7	8	5	1	6	9	2	3	4
6	9	2	4	3	5	1	7	8
4	3	1	7	8	2	5	9	6
3	6	9	8	5	1	7	4	2
2	1	4	9	7	6	3	8	5
5	7	8	3	2	4	9	6	1

6	8	9	1	4	2	3	7	5
7	2	1	3	9	5	8	4	6
4	3	5	6	7	8	9	2	1
5	9	8	2	3	4	6	1	7
1	4	2	8	6	7	5	3	9
3	6	7	5	1	9	2	8	4
8	7	4	9	2	6	1	5	3
9	5	3	7	8	1	4	6	2
2	1	6	4	5	3	7	9	8

3	1	5	7	8	6	2	9	4
4	7	6	2	1	9	3	8	5
8	2	9	4	3	5	7	1	6
2	5	1	3	7	8	6	4	9
7	3	8	9	6	4	5	2	1
9	6	4	5	2	1	8	3	7
1	9	3	8	5	7	4	6	2
5	4	2	6	9	3	1	7	8
6	8	7	1	4	2	9	5	3

3	4	7	2	1	9	8	5	6
9	2	1	5	6	8	4	7	3
6	8	5	3	7	4	2	9	1
8	5	6	7	2	3	9	1	4
1	7	9	8	4	5	6	3	2
2	3	4	1	9	6	7	8	5
5	9	2	6	3	7	1	4	8
7	6	3	4	8	1	5	2	9
4	1	8	9	5	2	3	6	7

8	7	9	5	6	1	3	4	2
1	3	6	4	8	2	9	5	7
2	4	5	9	7	3	8	6	1
7	9	8	3	1	4	5	2	6
3	5	1	6	2	9	4	7	8
4	6	2	7	5	8	1	3	9
5	8	3	2	9	6	7	1	4
6	1	4	8	3	7	2	9	5
9	2	7	1	4	5	6	8	3

9	4	5	3	8	2	1	7	6
2	1	7	4	9	6	3	8	5
8	6	3	7	1	5	2	9	4
6	9	8	5	7	1	4	3	2
1	7	2	6	3	4	8	5	9
3	5	4	8	2	9	7	6	1
4	8	6	1	5	7	9	2	3
5	3	9	2	4	8	6	1	7
7	2	1	9	6	3	5	4	8

1	9	3	4	8	5	7	6	2
8	4	5	6	2	7	3	1	9
7	6	2	9	3	1	4	5	8
5	1	7	2	6	3	8	9	4
2	8	4	5	1	9	6	3	7
9	3	6	7	4	8	5	2	1
3	7	9	8	5	2	1	4	6
4	5	8	1	9	6	2	7	3
6	2	1	3	7	4	9	8	5

9	5	8	6	4	3	2	1	7
3	7	2	9	8	1	4	5	6
6	4	1	5	2	7	3	9	8
1	9	7	4	5	8	6	3	2
5	8	6	1	3	2	7	4	9
2	3	4	7	9	6	1	8	5
4	2	3	8	6	5	9	7	1
7	6	5	3	1	9	8	2	4
8	1	9	2	7	4	5	6	3

3	8	6	2	1	4	9	7	5
7	5	2	9	3	8	4	1	6
1	9	4	7	6	5	2	3	8
9	4	3	6	8	2	7	5	1
5	6	8	4	7	1	3	2	9
2	1	7	3	5	9	8	6	4
6	2	9	1	4	3	5	8	7
4	7	5	8	2	6	1	9	3
8	3	1	5	9	7	6	4	2

9	8	6	1	4	5	7	3	2
3	2	4	9	6	7	5	1	8
7	1	5	2	8	3	4	9	6
1	4	9	5	7	6	2	8	3
6	3	8	4	2	1	9	5	7
5	7	2	3	9	8	6	4	1
4	6	7	8	3	9	1	2	5
8	9	1	7	5	2	3	6	4
2	5	3	6	1	4	8	7	9

9	5	1	4	8	6	3	7	2
3	2	4	1	7	9	8	6	5
7	8	6	5	2	3	9	4	1
6	7	9	2	4	8	5	1	3
2	4	3	9	5	1	7	8	6
8	1	5	6	3	7	4	2	9
1	9	8	3	6	4	2	5	7
4	6	2	7	9	5	1	3	8
5	3	7	8	1	2	6	9	4

4	1	7	8	9	5	3	2	6
3	8	2	1	6	4	7	5	9
5	9	6	7	3	2	8	1	4
9	6	8	5	2	3	1	4	7
2	7	4	9	1	6	5	8	3
1	3	5	4	8	7	6	9	2
7	2	9	3	5	8	4	6	1
6	5	3	2	4	1	9	7	8
8	4	1	6	7	9	2	3	5

8	7	5	6	1	3	4	2	9
2	4	3	8	7	9	5	1	6
1	9	6	5	2	4	7	3	8
6	1	7	9	8	2	3	5	4
5	3	2	4	6	1	9	8	7
4	8	9	3	5	7	2	6	1
7	5	1	2	9	6	8	4	3
3	6	8	7	4	5	1	9	2
9	2	4	1	3	8	6	7	5

6	2	8	9	4	1	7	5	3
9	1	4	5	3	7	8	6	2
7	5	3	6	2	8	4	9	1
5	8	2	4	7	9	1	3	6
4	9	7	3	1	6	2	8	5
1	3	6	8	5	2	9	4	7
8	7	5	1	9	3	6	2	4
3	6	1	2	8	4	5	7	9
2	4	9	7	6	5	3	1	8

2	1	6	7	5	3	8	4	9
8	7	9	1	4	6	2	5	3
3	4	5	2	9	8	7	1	6
4	5	1	9	3	7	6	2	8
7	3	8	5	6	2	4	9	1
6	9	2	4	8	1	5	3	7
5	8	3	6	1	4	9	7	2
9	6	7	3	2	5	1	8	4
1	2	4	8	7	9	3	6	5

3	6	2	7	9	5	4	1	8
4	5	7	1	8	2	6	9	3
1	9	8	3	4	6	7	2	5
2	3	9	5	7	4	1	8	6
6	8	1	9	2	3	5	4	7
7	4	5	8	6	1	2	3	9
5	7	4	2	3	8	9	6	1
8	1	6	4	5	9	3	7	2
9	2	3	6	1	7	8	5	4

3	5	8	4	6	1	9	2	7
9	2	7	5	3	8	6	1	4
4	6	1	2	7	9	8	5	3
1	8	4	3	9	7	5	6	2
2	3	6	8	5	4	7	9	1
7	9	5	6	1	2	4	3	8
6	7	9	1	4	3	2	8	5
8	4	3	9	2	5	1	7	6
5	1	2	7	8	6	3	4	9

1	7	2	4	6	9	8	5	3
6	4	3	1	5	8	2	9	7
9	5	8	7	3	2	1	6	4
7	8	6	2	9	4	5	3	1
3	2	4	8	1	5	6	7	9
5	1	9	3	7	6	4	8	2
4	3	5	6	2	7	9	1	8
2	9	1	5	8	3	7	4	6
8	6	7	9	4	1	3	2	5

3	4	1	9	2	6	7	8	5
7	6	8	4	5	3	1	2	9
5	9	2	1	7	8	4	6	3
1	2	9	8	4	5	6	3	7
6	5	3	2	1	7	8	9	4
4	8	7	3	6	9	5	1	2
2	7	6	5	3	1	9	4	8
9	1	4	7	8	2	3	5	6
8	3	5	6	9	4	2	7	1

8	6	2	7	9	4	3	5	1
3	4	7	1	8	5	6	2	9
1	5	9	3	2	6	8	4	7
5	9	4	2	3	8	7	1	6
7	8	3	5	6	1	2	9	4
2	1	6	4	7	9	5	8	3
4	2	5	6	1	3	9	7	8
6	7	8	9	4	2	1	3	5
9	3	1	8	5	7	4	6	2

5	8	9	2	6	4	3	1	7
3	7	2	1	9	8	5	4	6
4	6	1	7	5	3	2	8	9
9	1	5	4	7	6	8	2	3
2	3	7	8	1	9	4	6	5
6	4	8	3	2	5	7	9	1
8	5	4	9	3	1	6	7	2
7	9	3	6	4	2	1	5	8
1	2	6	5	8	7	9	3	4

7	4	3	6	5	9	1	8	2
6	8	1	2	3	4	7	5	9
5	9	2	8	7	1	3	4	6
8	7	4	1	2	6	5	9	3
9	2	6	3	4	5	8	7	1
1	3	5	7	9	8	6	2	4
2	5	8	4	1	3	9	6	7
3	6	7	9	8	2	4	1	5
4	1	9	5	6	7	2	3	8

8	7	3	2	5	9	6	4	1
6	4	1	3	7	8	5	9	2
2	9	5	6	4	1	7	8	3
5	6	7	8	9	2	1	3	4
1	3	2	5	6	4	8	7	9
4	8	9	1	3	7	2	5	6
9	2	6	4	8	5	3	1	7
7	1	8	9	2	3	4	6	5
3	5	4	7	1	6	9	2	8

6	9	4	7	5	3	2	1	8
1	7	8	6	4	2	5	9	3
2	5	3	9	8	1	7	6	4
4	1	5	3	7	6	8	2	9
8	3	2	4	1	9	6	5	7
7	6	9	5	2	8	3	4	1
5	2	1	8	3	4	9	7	6
3	4	6	2	9	7	1	8	5
9	8	7	1	6	5	4	3	2

9	5	6	2	7	8	1	4	3
2	4	3	1	6	9	8	5	7
1	8	7	3	5	4	9	2	6
6	9	1	4	2	7	3	8	5
3	2	5	9	8	1	6	7	4
4	7	8	5	3	6	2	1	9
5	6	4	8	1	3	7	9	2
8	3	9	7	4	2	5	6	1
7	1	2	6	9	5	4	3	8

8	1	4	2	5	3	7	9	6
9	5	3	8	7	6	2	1	4
6	2	7	9	1	4	8	3	5
3	6	2	5	8	7	9	4	1
1	4	5	6	9	2	3	8	7
7	8	9	4	3	1	6	5	2
4	7	8	3	2	5	1	6	9
5	9	1	7	6	8	4	2	3
2	3	6	1	4	9	5	7	8

3	2	9	5	7	1	8	4	6
1	6	5	4	3	8	7	2	9
7	4	8	6	2	9	5	3	1
4	5	2	8	9	3	6	1	7
8	7	1	2	4	6	9	5	3
6	9	3	7	1	5	4	8	2
5	1	6	9	8	2	3	7	4
2	8	7	3	6	4	1	9	5
9	3	4	1	5	7	2	6	8

7	1	9	3	4	6	8	5	2
8	5	6	9	7	2	1	3	4
2	4	3	5	8	1	7	6	9
4	7	1	8	2	3	6	9	5
5	9	8	7	6	4	3	2	1
3	6	2	1	9	5	4	8	7
6	2	5	4	3	7	9	1	8
1	8	4	6	5	9	2	7	3
9	3	7	2	1	8	5	4	6

9	7	1	2	8	6	3	4	5
8	4	2	9	5	3	1	6	7
6	3	5	1	4	7	8	9	2
7	2	4	5	6	8	9	3	1
3	1	9	4	7	2	6	5	8
5	8	6	3	1	9	2	7	4
4	6	7	8	9	1	5	2	3
1	5	3	6	2	4	7	8	9
2	9	8	7	3	5	4	1	6

5	1	4	6	7	8	3	2	9
9	7	6	2	5	3	4	8	1
3	2	8	9	4	1	6	7	5
2	9	3	1	6	4	8	5	7
4	6	5	8	2	7	1	9	3
7	8	1	5	3	9	2	6	4
1	3	9	7	8	6	5	4	2
6	5	7	4	1	2	9	3	8
8	4	2	3	9	5	7	1	6

5	1	7	9	8	4	2	6	3
9	2	4	3	7	6	5	8	1
3	8	6	1	2	5	7	9	4
7	4	5	8	9	1	6	3	2
2	3	1	4	6	7	8	5	9
6	9	8	5	3	2	4	1	7
4	7	9	6	5	3	1	2	8
1	6	3	2	4	8	9	7	5
8	5	2	7	1	9	3	4	6

6	1	4	5	3	8	2	7	9
2	8	5	1	7	9	6	4	3
9	7	3	4	2	6	1	5	8
5	9	7	8	1	4	3	2	6
3	4	2	6	9	7	8	1	5
8	6	1	3	5	2	4	9	7
1	2	9	7	8	3	5	6	4
4	5	8	9	6	1	7	3	2
7	3	6	2	4	5	9	8	1

9	4	7	5	6	1	8	3	2
8	2	1	9	7	3	4	5	6
5	3	6	8	2	4	9	7	1
4	1	2	3	9	7	5	6	8
6	9	5	2	1	8	7	4	3
3	7	8	4	5	6	2	1	9
1	6	9	7	4	2	3	8	5
2	8	4	1	3	5	6	9	7
7	5	3	6	8	9	1	2	4

1	6	2	3	5	8	7	4	9
4	3	7	2	6	9	1	8	5
8	9	5	1	4	7	3	6	2
6	8	9	4	2	3	5	1	7
7	2	4	9	1	5	8	3	6
5	1	3	7	8	6	9	2	4
2	7	6	8	9	1	4	5	3
3	4	8	5	7	2	6	9	1
9	5	1	6	3	4	2	7	8

2	1	4	7	5	6	3	8	9
7	3	9	1	8	4	2	5	6
5	6	8	3	2	9	1	4	7
4	9	7	8	6	3	5	1	2
6	5	3	4	1	2	9	7	8
1	8	2	5	9	7	6	3	4
9	4	5	6	3	8	7	2	1
3	7	6	2	4	1	8	9	5
8	2	1	9	7	5	4	6	3

4	1	8	9	3	5	6	7	2
5	2	7	1	8	6	4	9	3
3	9	6	2	7	4	1	5	8
6	4	3	8	5	7	9	2	1
7	5	9	3	1	2	8	6	4
1	8	2	4	6	9	7	3	5
8	3	5	7	9	1	2	4	6
9	6	4	5	2	8	3	1	7
2	7	1	6	4	3	5	8	9

2	5	8	3	1	9	7	4	6
3	4	9	5	7	6	1	2	8
7	1	6	8	2	4	5	3	9
5	7	4	9	3	1	6	8	2
1	6	2	7	4	8	9	5	3
9	8	3	2	6	5	4	1	7
4	2	7	6	5	3	8	9	1
6	9	1	4	8	2	3	7	5
8	3	5	1	9	7	2	6	4

5	3	7	4	8	1	9	6	2
2	8	1	5	9	6	7	4	3
9	6	4	3	2	7	1	8	5
4	5	2	6	7	3	8	1	9
8	7	9	1	4	2	3	5	6
6	1	3	8	5	9	4	2	7
1	4	6	7	3	5	2	9	8
7	9	8	2	6	4	5	3	1
3	2	5	9	1	8	6	7	4

2	7	6	8	1	3	9	5	4
5	4	1	6	7	9	3	2	8
9	3	8	5	2	4	6	7	1
8	9	7	2	6	1	5	4	3
3	2	5	7	4	8	1	9	6
6	1	4	9	3	5	2	8	7
1	5	3	4	9	7	8	6	2
7	6	9	1	8	2	4	3	5
4	8	2	3	5	6	7	1	9

5	6	8	7	2	4	9	3	1
2	7	9	1	6	3	8	4	5
4	3	1	5	8	9	6	7	2
6	9	2	4	3	8	1	5	7
8	5	3	6	7	1	4	2	9
1	4	7	9	5	2	3	8	6
3	1	6	2	4	5	7	9	8
9	8	5	3	1	7	2	6	4
7	2	4	8	9	6	5	1	3

7	1	4	8	6	2	3	5	9
2	6	5	3	4	9	7	8	1
9	3	8	5	7	1	6	4	2
6	7	9	4	8	3	2	1	5
5	4	3	2	1	6	9	7	8
1	8	2	9	5	7	4	3	6
3	9	7	1	2	8	5	6	4
8	5	6	7	9	4	1	2	3
4	2	1	6	3	5	8	9	7

5	7	6	2	3	8	9	1	4
3	4	1	9	5	7	6	8	2
9	2	8	6	4	1	3	7	5
7	8	2	4	6	5	1	3	9
4	1	3	8	9	2	7	5	6
6	5	9	1	7	3	2	4	8
8	6	5	3	1	9	4	2	7
1	9	7	5	2	4	8	6	3
2	3	4	7	8	6	5	9	1

4	5	8	7	6	1	3	9	2
6	2	3	5	9	4	7	8	1
1	7	9	2	3	8	5	6	4
3	1	4	6	2	9	8	5	7
2	9	6	8	5	7	4	1	3
7	8	5	4	1	3	6	2	9
8	4	2	1	7	6	9	3	5
5	3	7	9	8	2	1	4	6
9	6	1	3	4	5	2	7	8

4	9	7	6	2	8	1	5	3
6	5	3	4	7	1	9	8	2
2	8	1	5	9	3	6	7	4
3	2	8	7	5	9	4	6	1
5	4	6	1	8	2	3	9	7
1	7	9	3	6	4	5	2	8
7	3	2	9	1	6	8	4	5
9	1	5	8	4	7	2	3	6
8	6	4	2	3	5	7	1	9

3	7	6	8	1	9	4	5	2
2	4	5	7	6	3	9	8	1
8	1	9	2	5	4	3	6	7
4	9	7	6	3	5	2	1	8
5	3	8	9	2	1	7	4	6
6	2	1	4	8	7	5	3	9
9	6	2	3	4	8	1	7	5
7	5	4	1	9	6	8	2	3
1	8	3	5	7	2	6	9	4

8	1	2	4	6	5	3	9	7
9	6	5	3	8	7	4	1	2
7	3	4	9	1	2	8	5	6
4	2	8	7	3	1	9	6	5
6	5	7	8	2	9	1	4	3
3	9	1	6	5	4	2	7	8
2	4	3	1	7	6	5	8	9
1	8	6	5	9	3	7	2	4
5	7	9	2	4	8	6	3	1

2	7	5	6	3	4	8	9	1
1	6	9	8	7	5	3	4	2
8	4	3	9	1	2	5	7	6
9	1	2	4	5	8	6	3	7
4	5	7	2	6	3	1	8	9
3	8	6	7	9	1	4	2	5
7	9	1	3	4	6	2	5	8
5	3	8	1	2	7	9	6	4
6	2	4	5	8	9	7	1	3

4	5	6	9	3	2	8	7	1
3	2	8	4	1	7	6	5	9
9	1	7	5	8	6	4	3	2
2	7	3	8	6	9	5	1	4
5	8	1	3	2	4	7	9	6
6	9	4	7	5	1	3	2	8
7	4	2	6	9	3	1	8	5
1	6	5	2	7	8	9	4	3
8	3	9	1	4	5	2	6	7

9	4	1	5	6	3	8	7	2
7	6	2	8	4	1	5	9	3
3	5	8	9	7	2	1	6	4
4	2	6	7	1	5	3	8	9
1	7	9	2	3	8	4	5	6
5	8	3	4	9	6	2	1	7
8	3	7	6	5	4	9	2	1
6	1	5	3	2	9	7	4	8
2	9	4	1	8	7	6	3	5

9	7	2	6	4	1	3	8	5
6	3	1	8	5	7	9	4	2
4	8	5	3	9	2	1	6	7
2	9	8	1	3	4	7	5	6
1	4	7	9	6	5	8	2	3
3	5	6	2	7	8	4	9	1
5	1	9	7	8	6	2	3	4
8	2	4	5	1	3	6	7	9
7	6	3	4	2	9	5	1	8

6	2	9	5	4	3	1	8	7
5	4	8	7	6	1	9	2	3
7	1	3	9	2	8	4	5	6
2	5	1	4	3	6	8	7	9
9	8	6	2	5	7	3	1	4
3	7	4	1	8	9	2	6	5
4	9	7	8	1	5	6	3	2
1	3	2	6	7	4	5	9	8
8	6	5	3	9	2	7	4	1

5	4	7	8	3	9	2	6	1
1	6	3	4	7	2	5	8	9
2	9	8	5	6	1	4	7	3
4	8	6	7	1	5	9	3	2
7	1	2	9	4	3	8	5	6
9	3	5	2	8	6	1	4	7
3	5	1	6	2	4	7	9	8
6	7	4	1	9	8	3	2	5
8	2	9	3	5	7	6	1	4

4	7	3	2	5	8	1	9	6
6	1	5	4	7	9	2	8	3
2	9	8	1	6	3	5	4	7
9	5	1	7	8	6	3	2	4
8	4	7	5	3	2	6	1	9
3	2	6	9	4	1	7	5	8
1	6	4	8	2	7	9	3	5
5	3	2	6	9	4	8	7	1
7	8	9	3	1	5	4	6	2

1	8	2	9	4	5	7	6	3
4	9	3	8	6	7	5	2	1
6	5	7	1	2	3	9	8	4
7	4	6	3	1	9	2	5	8
2	1	8	6	5	4	3	7	9
5	3	9	2	7	8	1	4	6
3	6	1	7	8	2	4	9	5
9	2	5	4	3	6	8	1	7
8	7	4	5	9	1	6	3	2

9	8	1	7	6	5	2	3	4
6	4	3	1	8	2	7	5	9
2	5	7	9	3	4	6	1	8
4	1	5	8	2	6	9	7	3
8	7	9	5	1	3	4	6	2
3	6	2	4	7	9	5	8	1
5	9	8	3	4	7	1	2	6
1	2	4	6	5	8	3	9	7
7	3	6	2	9	1	8	4	5

7	8	9	3	6	2	1	5	4
5	4	1	9	7	8	6	2	3
6	3	2	1	4	5	7	9	8
1	6	7	2	3	9	4	8	5
4	2	5	7	8	6	3	1	9
8	9	3	4	5	1	2	7	6
9	7	6	5	2	4	8	3	1
3	1	4	8	9	7	5	6	2
2	5	8	6	1	3	9	4	7

7	9	4	2	8	3	6	5	1
6	3	2	7	5	1	8	4	9
8	5	1	9	6	4	3	7	2
3	1	9	8	7	5	2	6	4
4	6	8	3	9	2	7	1	5
2	7	5	4	1	6	9	8	3
9	8	3	1	4	7	5	2	6
1	2	6	5	3	8	4	9	7
5	4	7	6	2	9	1	3	8

3	6	2	4	7	8	9	1	5
8	1	9	2	6	5	4	3	7
7	5	4	3	9	1	6	8	2
4	2	7	1	3	6	5	9	8
9	8	6	7	5	4	3	2	1
1	3	5	9	8	2	7	4	6
2	9	8	6	4	7	1	5	3
5	7	3	8	1	9	2	6	4
6	4	1	5	2	3	8	7	9

1	5	8	3	9	6	7	2	4
4	9	2	5	7	1	6	8	3
3	7	6	4	2	8	5	1	9
7	4	3	6	8	5	1	9	2
8	6	5	2	1	9	3	4	7
9	2	1	7	4	3	8	5	6
6	8	4	1	3	2	9	7	5
5	1	7	9	6	4	2	3	8
2	3	9	8	5	7	4	6	1

2	8	9	4	1	5	6	3	7
3	6	4	8	2	7	1	5	9
5	1	7	6	9	3	8	2	4
7	5	3	9	4	6	2	8	1
9	4	8	1	3	2	5	7	6
1	2	6	7	5	8	9	4	3
6	7	1	2	8	4	3	9	5
4	3	2	5	6	9	7	1	8
8	9	5	3	7	1	4	6	2

2	6	4	5	9	8	1	7	3
8	7	5	2	1	3	6	9	4
9	3	1	6	4	7	5	2	8
1	5	2	9	7	4	3	8	6
7	9	3	1	8	6	4	5	2
4	8	6	3	5	2	9	1	7
5	4	8	7	6	9	2	3	1
3	1	7	4	2	5	8	6	9
6	2	9	8	3	1	7	4	5

2	4	8	6	3	5	9	7	1
1	5	6	2	7	9	4	3	8
7	3	9	4	8	1	2	5	6
9	6	3	1	4	2	5	8	7
5	1	7	9	6	8	3	2	4
4	8	2	3	5	7	1	6	9
8	9	4	5	2	6	7	1	3
6	2	1	7	9	3	8	4	5
3	7	5	8	1	4	6	9	2

2	7	8	5	4	6	3	9	1
6	1	5	8	3	9	2	7	4
4	9	3	2	1	7	6	8	5
8	6	7	1	5	2	4	3	9
5	4	2	6	9	3	8	1	7
9	3	1	7	8	4	5	2	6
7	2	9	3	6	5	1	4	8
3	8	6	4	7	1	9	5	2
1	5	4	9	2	8	7	6	3

5	8	6	3	2	4	9	1	7
7	3	1	6	5	9	2	4	8
4	2	9	1	7	8	6	3	5
1	5	2	9	8	7	3	6	4
9	7	8	4	3	6	1	5	2
3	6	4	2	1	5	7	8	9
8	4	3	7	9	1	5	2	6
2	9	5	8	6	3	4	7	1
6	1	7	5	4	2	8	9	3

1	8	4	3	6	7	5	9	2
6	7	9	1	2	5	3	4	8
2	5	3	9	8	4	6	7	1
8	1	5	6	9	2	4	3	7
3	9	7	4	5	8	2	1	6
4	2	6	7	1	3	8	5	9
7	6	2	5	4	9	1	8	3
9	4	1	8	3	6	7	2	5
5	3	8	2	7	1	9	6	4

6	4	2	3	8	9	5	7	1
8	3	9	7	1	5	4	2	6
5	1	7	2	4	6	9	8	3
2	6	4	8	5	1	7	3	9
9	7	1	6	2	3	8	4	5
3	8	5	4	9	7	6	1	2
1	2	8	5	6	4	3	9	7
4	5	3	9	7	2	1	6	8
7	9	6	1	3	8	2	5	4

2	1	7	9	4	3	5	8	6
6	3	5	2	1	8	7	9	4
8	9	4	5	7	6	2	1	3
1	8	2	3	6	5	9	4	7
3	4	6	8	9	7	1	5	2
5	7	9	1	2	4	6	3	8
9	5	3	6	8	2	4	7	1
4	6	8	7	5	1	3	2	9
7	2	1	4	3	9	8	6	5

7	4	2	1	6	8	9	3	5
5	1	3	4	9	2	6	7	8
8	6	9	5	3	7	4	1	2
1	3	5	7	2	9	8	6	4
6	9	7	8	1	4	5	2	3
2	8	4	3	5	6	1	9	7
9	5	1	2	4	3	7	8	6
4	2	8	6	7	1	3	5	9
3	7	6	9	8	5	2	4	1

1	8	5	4	7	2	3	9	6
2	7	4	3	6	9	1	8	5
6	9	3	5	1	8	2	7	4
8	3	1	9	4	5	7	6	2
4	2	6	8	3	7	5	1	9
7	5	9	1	2	6	8	4	3
5	6	7	2	9	1	4	3	8
9	4	8	7	5	3	6	2	1
3	1	2	6	8	4	9	5	7

3	9	8	6	2	1	4	5	7
5	6	7	4	3	9	1	8	2
2	4	1	5	8	7	9	6	3
4	1	5	3	6	2	8	7	9
8	3	2	7	9	4	5	1	6
6	7	9	1	5	8	3	2	4
9	8	4	2	1	6	7	3	5
1	5	6	9	7	3	2	4	8
7	2	3	8	4	5	6	9	1

9	6	7	4	2	3	8	5	1
2	1	8	5	7	6	9	3	4
4	5	3	9	1	8	6	7	2
3	4	6	1	5	2	7	9	8
8	7	2	6	3	9	4	1	5
5	9	1	7	8	4	3	2	6
6	2	4	3	9	5	1	8	7
1	3	5	8	6	7	2	4	9
7	8	9	2	4	1	5	6	3

7	8	2	6	9	5	4	1	3
1	9	3	2	4	8	7	5	6
4	6	5	7	3	1	2	9	8
9	5	7	4	8	3	1	6	2
2	3	8	1	7	6	5	4	9
6	1	4	5	2	9	3	8	7
5	2	9	8	1	7	6	3	4
8	7	6	3	5	4	9	2	1
3	4	1	9	6	2	8	7	5

6	2	3	7	8	9	1	4	5
8	7	5	2	1	4	3	9	6
9	1	4	6	5	3	7	8	2
3	4	8	9	7	5	6	2	1
7	5	2	4	6	1	8	3	9
1	9	6	8	3	2	4	5	7
4	6	9	3	2	7	5	1	8
5	3	7	1	9	8	2	6	4
2	8	1	5	4	6	9	7	3

5	7	8	3	1	9	6	2	4
1	9	3	2	6	4	5	8	7
4	6	2	8	5	7	9	1	3
6	5	1	4	3	8	2	7	9
2	3	4	7	9	6	1	5	8
9	8	7	1	2	5	3	4	6
7	2	9	5	8	3	4	6	1
8	1	6	9	4	2	7	3	5
3	4	5	6	7	1	8	9	2

1	4	9	6	8	7	5	2	3
7	6	8	3	2	5	9	4	1
2	5	3	9	4	1	8	7	6
5	7	6	8	1	4	2	3	9
3	8	2	5	6	9	7	1	4
9	1	4	7	3	2	6	5	8
4	3	5	2	9	6	1	8	7
6	2	1	4	7	8	3	9	5
8	9	7	1	5	3	4	6	2

1	8	5	4	6	7	2	9	3
9	7	2	3	8	1	4	5	6
4	6	3	9	5	2	8	7	1
8	5	6	1	3	9	7	4	2
7	2	9	5	4	6	1	3	8
3	4	1	2	7	8	9	6	5
2	3	8	7	9	5	6	1	4
5	1	7	6	2	4	3	8	9
6	9	4	8	1	3	5	2	7

7	1	3	6	9	8	5	4	2
4	2	6	3	1	5	9	7	8
8	5	9	7	2	4	6	1	3
2	8	7	4	6	3	1	9	5
5	9	4	2	7	1	3	8	6
6	3	1	8	5	9	7	2	4
3	7	8	1	4	6	2	5	9
9	6	2	5	8	7	4	3	1
1	4	5	9	3	2	8	6	7

9	2	6	3	4	7	1	8	5
5	7	3	2	8	1	6	9	4
4	8	1	9	6	5	3	7	2
2	3	9	6	1	4	8	5	7
6	1	8	7	5	9	4	2	3
7	5	4	8	2	3	9	6	1
3	6	7	4	9	2	5	1	8
1	9	2	5	3	8	7	4	6
8	4	5	1	7	6	2	3	9

2	1	7	9	8	3	4	6	5
5	8	6	1	7	4	3	9	2
9	3	4	6	5	2	1	8	7
4	9	1	5	3	6	2	7	8
7	5	8	4	2	1	9	3	6
6	2	3	7	9	8	5	1	4
8	7	9	3	4	5	6	2	1
1	4	2	8	6	9	7	5	3
3	6	5	2	1	7	8	4	9

5	2	7	4	8	1	6	3	9
8	4	1	9	6	3	2	5	7
9	6	3	7	2	5	8	1	4
2	9	6	5	4	7	1	8	3
4	1	8	2	3	9	7	6	5
7	3	5	6	1	8	4	9	2
6	7	9	1	5	4	3	2	8
3	5	2	8	7	6	9	4	1
1	8	4	3	9	2	5	7	6

4	5	6	9	1	2	3	8	7
9	1	2	3	8	7	6	4	5
7	3	8	6	5	4	9	2	1
6	9	1	5	2	3	4	7	8
3	2	7	4	6	8	1	5	9
8	4	5	1	7	9	2	3	6
1	8	9	2	4	5	7	6	3
5	6	4	7	3	1	8	9	2
2	7	3	8	9	6	5	1	4

3	9	2	5	7	8	6	4	1
6	8	1	9	3	4	5	7	2
5	4	7	6	1	2	3	9	8
4	2	8	7	6	1	9	3	5
9	5	6	8	2	3	7	1	4
7	1	3	4	9	5	8	2	6
8	3	4	1	5	9	2	6	7
2	7	5	3	4	6	1	8	9
1	6	9	2	8	7	4	5	3

3	5	2	8	6	4	7	1	9
7	4	6	1	2	9	8	5	3
8	1	9	7	3	5	2	4	6
9	2	4	5	8	1	6	3	7
1	3	8	2	7	6	4	9	5
6	7	5	9	4	3	1	8	2
4	8	7	3	9	2	5	6	1
2	9	1	6	5	8	3	7	4
5	6	3	4	1	7	9	2	8

5	3	2	4	7	9	8	1	6
9	4	7	8	1	6	5	2	3
8	1	6	3	5	2	4	7	9
3	7	4	9	2	5	6	8	1
2	5	1	6	8	3	9	4	7
6	8	9	1	4	7	2	3	5
1	6	3	2	9	8	7	5	4
7	9	8	5	3	4	1	6	2
4	2	5	7	6	1	3	9	8

8	1	7	5	4	2	9	3	6
6	5	9	7	3	1	8	4	2
2	3	4	8	9	6	7	5	1
1	6	5	3	2	8	4	7	9
7	8	2	4	5	9	6	1	3
9	4	3	6	1	7	2	8	5
4	2	1	9	8	5	3	6	7
3	9	6	1	7	4	5	2	8
5	7	8	2	6	3	1	9	4

8	6	3	2	1	7	5	9	4
7	9	4	6	5	3	8	1	2
2	1	5	9	4	8	7	3	6
5	3	6	1	7	9	4	2	8
4	7	8	3	6	2	1	5	9
9	2	1	5	8	4	3	6	7
1	4	2	7	9	5	6	8	3
6	8	9	4	3	1	2	7	5
3	5	7	8	2	6	9	4	1

3	4	8	1	9	5	2	6	7
2	1	5	7	8	6	3	9	4
6	9	7	3	2	4	5	1	8
5	2	3	9	4	1	8	7	6
7	8	1	6	5	3	4	2	9
4	6	9	8	7	2	1	3	5
8	7	2	5	1	9	6	4	3
9	3	4	2	6	8	7	5	1
1	5	6	4	3	7	9	8	2

2	3	1	4	5	7	6	9	8
5	7	6	1	9	8	4	2	3
8	4	9	3	6	2	1	7	5
3	9	5	2	7	4	8	1	6
7	1	8	9	3	6	2	5	4
4	6	2	8	1	5	9	3	7
9	5	7	6	8	1	3	4	2
1	8	4	7	2	3	5	6	9
6	2	3	5	4	9	7	8	1

8	2	1	9	3	6	5	4	7
4	9	6	5	8	7	1	2	3
3	7	5	1	4	2	6	8	9
6	3	4	8	2	9	7	1	5
5	8	9	3	7	1	4	6	2
7	1	2	4	6	5	3	9	8
2	4	7	6	5	8	9	3	1
9	6	8	7	1	3	2	5	4
1	5	3	2	9	4	8	7	6

9	8	1	4	2	6	5	7	3
5	3	6	7	9	1	2	8	4
4	7	2	8	5	3	6	9	1
6	4	5	9	3	8	7	1	2
3	9	7	6	1	2	8	4	5
2	1	8	5	7	4	3	6	9
8	6	3	2	4	9	1	5	7
1	5	9	3	6	7	4	2	8
7	2	4	1	8	5	9	3	6

3	5	1	6	9	7	4	2	8
8	2	7	5	4	1	3	9	6
6	9	4	2	8	3	7	5	1
5	3	8	9	6	2	1	7	4
7	4	2	1	3	8	9	6	5
9	1	6	4	7	5	8	3	2
1	8	9	3	5	6	2	4	7
4	7	5	8	2	9	6	1	3
2	6	3	7	1	4	5	8	9

4	7	2	5	9	1	6	8	3
3	6	9	8	2	4	7	1	5
8	1	5	7	6	3	4	2	9
9	3	7	1	8	5	2	6	4
1	2	6	9	4	7	3	5	8
5	8	4	6	3	2	1	9	7
7	9	3	2	1	8	5	4	6
2	5	8	4	7	6	9	3	1
6	4	1	3	5	9	8	7	2

6	8	5	1	7	3	2	4	9
2	1	4	5	6	9	8	3	7
7	9	3	8	4	2	5	6	1
5	6	1	3	8	4	7	9	2
8	4	7	2	9	6	1	5	3
3	2	9	7	1	5	6	8	4
4	3	2	6	5	1	9	7	8
9	7	6	4	2	8	3	1	5
1	5	8	9	3	7	4	2	6

8	4	7	9	2	1	5	6	3
1	3	9	8	5	6	4	7	2
6	5	2	3	4	7	1	8	9
5	8	3	7	1	4	9	2	6
9	7	1	2	6	8	3	4	5
2	6	4	5	9	3	7	1	8
4	2	5	1	8	9	6	3	7
3	1	8	6	7	5	2	9	4
7	9	6	4	3	2	8	5	1

5	4	7	9	3	8	2	1	6
1	8	2	5	7	6	4	9	3
6	3	9	2	1	4	7	8	5
7	1	6	8	9	5	3	2	4
2	5	3	6	4	1	8	7	9
8	9	4	3	2	7	6	5	1
4	7	8	1	6	9	5	3	2
9	2	5	4	8	3	1	6	7
3	6	1	7	5	2	9	4	8

2	7	4	3	8	6	1	9	5
6	9	5	1	7	2	4	3	8
3	1	8	5	4	9	6	2	7
4	5	1	8	3	7	9	6	2
7	3	9	2	6	5	8	1	4
8	6	2	9	1	4	5	7	3
5	2	3	4	9	1	7	8	6
1	8	7	6	5	3	2	4	9
9	4	6	7	2	8	3	5	1

1	9	6	4	3	2	8	5	7
5	2	4	7	9	8	3	1	6
8	7	3	6	1	5	4	2	9
6	1	7	2	5	4	9	3	8
4	5	8	3	6	9	1	7	2
9	3	2	8	7	1	5	6	4
2	8	5	1	4	6	7	9	3
3	6	9	5	8	7	2	4	1
7	4	1	9	2	3	6	8	5

9	3	6	4	2	1	7	8	5
7	8	1	3	9	5	2	6	4
2	4	5	8	7	6	1	9	3
8	5	3	6	4	2	9	7	1
1	7	2	9	5	8	3	4	6
6	9	4	7	1	3	8	5	2
5	6	7	2	3	9	4	1	8
3	1	9	5	8	4	6	2	7
4	2	8	1	6	7	5	3	9

8	5	1	6	3	4	7	9	2
9	6	2	7	1	5	4	3	8
7	4	3	2	9	8	6	1	5
6	2	5	9	7	1	8	4	3
1	3	9	4	8	6	5	2	7
4	8	7	5	2	3	9	6	1
5	9	8	3	4	2	1	7	6
3	7	6	1	5	9	2	8	4
2	1	4	8	6	7	3	5	9

9	4	1	5	3	8	7	2	6
3	6	2	4	7	9	1	8	5
8	7	5	6	1	2	4	3	9
6	5	8	1	4	7	2	9	3
4	2	9	8	5	3	6	7	1
1	3	7	2	9	6	5	4	8
7	8	4	3	6	5	9	1	2
5	1	3	9	2	4	8	6	7
2	9	6	7	8	1	3	5	4

9	1	2	3	7	8	6	5	4
8	4	3	5	6	1	2	9	7
6	5	7	2	9	4	8	1	3
4	3	9	8	2	6	1	7	5
7	2	5	1	3	9	4	6	8
1	8	6	7	4	5	3	2	9
3	9	8	6	1	7	5	4	2
5	6	4	9	8	2	7	3	1
2	7	1	4	5	3	9	8	6

5	7	1	4	3	6	9	2	8
9	6	3	8	7	2	4	1	5
4	8	2	5	1	9	7	3	6
3	2	6	7	4	5	8	9	1
1	5	8	2	9	3	6	7	4
7	9	4	1	6	8	3	5	2
6	4	9	3	2	1	5	8	7
2	3	5	6	8	7	1	4	9
8	1	7	9	5	4	2	6	3

7	2	4	9	8	1	3	5	6
8	6	3	7	4	5	2	1	9
1	9	5	6	3	2	7	8	4
2	3	6	5	7	4	8	9	1
5	1	7	8	6	9	4	2	3
9	4	8	1	2	3	6	7	5
6	5	2	4	9	8	1	3	7
3	7	1	2	5	6	9	4	8
4	8	9	3	1	7	5	6	2

6	9	5	2	1	4	7	8	3
4	7	1	9	8	3	5	2	6
8	2	3	6	5	7	4	9	1
1	5	4	8	9	6	3	7	2
7	6	2	1	3	5	8	4	9
3	8	9	4	7	2	6	1	5
5	3	8	7	2	9	1	6	4
2	4	7	3	6	1	9	5	8
9	1	6	5	4	8	2	3	7

1	2	6	5	4	8	3	7	9
3	8	4	9	6	7	2	5	1
7	9	5	2	1	3	4	8	6
2	7	1	6	3	5	8	9	4
6	5	8	1	9	4	7	2	3
4	3	9	7	8	2	1	6	5
5	6	3	8	7	1	9	4	2
8	1	2	4	5	9	6	3	7
9	4	7	3	2	6	5	1	8

1	8	3	2	4	5	6	7	9
6	2	7	1	8	9	4	3	5
9	4	5	7	3	6	1	8	2
8	6	2	3	5	4	7	9	1
3	7	4	6	9	1	5	2	8
5	9	1	8	2	7	3	4	6
4	3	8	5	1	2	9	6	7
2	1	6	9	7	3	8	5	4
7	5	9	4	6	8	2	1	3

1	8	4	5	2	7	9	6	3
9	3	6	8	4	1	7	5	2
5	7	2	3	9	6	8	1	4
3	9	7	4	1	8	5	2	6
6	4	1	9	5	2	3	8	7
2	5	8	6	7	3	1	4	9
7	2	3	1	8	4	6	9	5
8	6	9	2	3	5	4	7	1
4	1	5	7	6	9	2	3	8

4	2	6	1	9	8	7	3	5
9	3	5	7	4	6	1	8	2
8	7	1	3	2	5	4	6	9
6	9	3	8	7	1	2	5	4
5	8	4	9	6	2	3	7	1
7	1	2	4	5	3	8	9	6
3	5	7	2	1	9	6	4	8
1	6	8	5	3	4	9	2	7
2	4	9	6	8	7	5	1	3

5	4	1	6	9	3	2	7	8
2	6	8	1	4	7	3	5	9
7	3	9	2	8	5	4	6	1
9	2	6	5	3	4	1	8	7
3	5	7	9	1	8	6	4	2
8	1	4	7	2	6	5	9	3
4	7	2	3	5	9	8	1	6
6	8	3	4	7	1	9	2	5
1	9	5	8	6	2	7	3	4

3	9	5	1	4	2	7	6	8
4	8	2	6	3	7	5	1	9
7	1	6	8	9	5	2	4	3
6	3	9	4	2	8	1	5	7
5	7	8	3	1	6	4	9	2
2	4	1	7	5	9	8	3	6
9	2	3	5	8	4	6	7	1
1	5	7	2	6	3	9	8	4
8	6	4	9	7	1	3	2	5

2	5	6	7	8	9	1	3	4
4	9	3	2	1	5	8	7	6
8	7	1	3	4	6	9	5	2
9	1	2	4	7	8	3	6	5
5	8	4	9	6	3	7	2	1
3	6	7	5	2	1	4	8	9
7	4	5	1	3	2	6	9	8
1	2	8	6	9	7	5	4	3
6	3	9	8	5	4	2	1	7

2	4	1	3	6	8	5	9	7
6	9	7	4	1	5	2	3	8
3	8	5	9	7	2	1	6	4
9	6	2	5	3	7	4	8	1
4	1	3	2	8	6	7	5	9
5	7	8	1	4	9	3	2	6
7	3	6	8	2	1	9	4	5
1	2	9	6	5	4	8	7	3
8	5	4	7	9	3	6	1	2

8	3	5	2	9	6	1	4	7
6	4	7	1	8	5	2	3	9
1	9	2	7	4	3	8	6	5
5	7	6	3	1	2	9	8	4
2	1	4	8	6	9	5	7	3
9	8	3	4	5	7	6	1	2
7	5	9	6	3	8	4	2	1
4	2	8	5	7	1	3	9	6
3	6	1	9	2	4	7	5	8

5	4	3	6	1	2	8	7	9
2	6	7	9	3	8	5	1	4
9	1	8	4	7	5	3	2	6
6	5	4	2	9	3	7	8	1
1	8	9	7	5	6	2	4	3
7	3	2	1	8	4	9	6	5
4	9	5	8	2	1	6	3	7
8	7	6	3	4	9	1	5	2
3	2	1	5	6	7	4	9	8

6	2	3	4	9	1	7	8	5
4	8	7	2	6	5	1	3	9
1	5	9	3	8	7	4	6	2
8	3	4	5	2	6	9	7	1
7	1	2	9	4	8	6	5	3
9	6	5	1	7	3	2	4	8
2	4	8	6	5	9	3	1	7
3	7	6	8	1	2	5	9	4
5	9	1	7	3	4	8	2	6

5	9	6	4	3	7	2	1	8
4	1	8	9	6	2	3	5	7
7	2	3	8	1	5	6	9	4
9	5	1	2	4	3	8	7	6
3	6	4	5	7	8	9	2	1
2	8	7	6	9	1	5	4	3
1	4	5	3	2	6	7	8	9
6	7	2	1	8	9	4	3	5
8	3	9	7	5	4	1	6	2

7	6	5	2	9	3	4	1	8
3	4	1	7	6	8	2	5	9
8	2	9	4	5	1	6	3	7
1	7	4	3	8	5	9	6	2
6	9	8	1	7	2	3	4	5
5	3	2	6	4	9	7	8	1
9	5	7	8	3	4	1	2	6
4	1	6	5	2	7	8	9	3
2	8	3	9	1	6	5	7	4

3	8	1	2	6	5	7	9	4
7	5	6	1	9	4	8	2	3
4	2	9	8	3	7	6	1	5
1	6	4	5	7	8	9	3	2
2	9	8	3	4	6	5	7	1
5	7	3	9	1	2	4	8	6
8	4	2	7	5	1	3	6	9
9	1	5	6	8	3	2	4	7
6	3	7	4	2	9	1	5	8

3	1	4	5	9	6	7	8	2
9	2	6	7	1	8	4	3	5
5	8	7	3	2	4	9	1	6
8	6	1	2	4	3	5	7	9
4	3	9	8	5	7	6	2	1
7	5	2	9	6	1	3	4	8
1	9	3	6	7	2	8	5	4
2	7	5	4	8	9	1	6	3
6	4	8	1	3	5	2	9	7

8	2	1	6	3	4	7	5	9
3	4	7	9	8	5	2	6	1
5	9	6	1	2	7	3	4	8
4	8	3	7	6	2	1	9	5
2	6	9	5	4	1	8	7	3
1	7	5	3	9	8	6	2	4
6	1	2	4	5	3	9	8	7
9	3	4	8	7	6	5	1	2
7	5	8	2	1	9	4	3	6

3	5	1	9	7	6	4	8	2
8	7	6	1	2	4	3	5	9
4	9	2	3	8	5	7	1	6
5	2	9	7	1	8	6	4	3
1	8	7	4	6	3	2	9	5
6	4	3	2	5	9	8	7	1
9	6	5	8	3	7	1	2	4
2	3	8	5	4	1	9	6	7
7	1	4	6	9	2	5	3	8

2	5	1	8	6	4	9	3	7
8	6	7	5	3	9	2	4	1
9	3	4	7	2	1	5	6	8
6	7	5	2	1	8	3	9	4
3	8	9	6	4	5	7	1	2
1	4	2	9	7	3	6	8	5
5	2	8	4	9	6	1	7	3
4	1	6	3	5	7	8	2	9
7	9	3	1	8	2	4	5	6

6	1	4	3	8	5	2	9	7
5	9	8	7	2	6	3	4	1
7	2	3	9	1	4	5	6	8
2	4	7	8	3	9	1	5	6
3	5	6	4	7	1	8	2	9
1	8	9	6	5	2	4	7	3
9	3	1	5	4	7	6	8	2
8	6	5	2	9	3	7	1	4
4	7	2	1	6	8	9	3	5

6	5	8	9	7	3	2	4	1
2	3	9	1	8	4	7	6	5
7	1	4	5	2	6	9	8	3
1	4	7	8	9	5	3	2	6
8	9	2	3	6	1	4	5	7
3	6	5	7	4	2	8	1	9
4	7	3	6	1	8	5	9	2
9	2	6	4	5	7	1	3	8
5	8	1	2	3	9	6	7	4

5	6	2	8	1	3	4	9	7
9	7	8	2	4	5	6	3	1
4	1	3	9	6	7	5	8	2
6	9	7	3	8	1	2	4	5
3	5	4	6	2	9	1	7	8
8	2	1	5	7	4	9	6	3
7	8	6	1	9	2	3	5	4
1	4	5	7	3	6	8	2	9
2	3	9	4	5	8	7	1	6

2	8	1	6	9	4	5	3	7
6	3	4	7	1	5	9	2	8
9	5	7	8	3	2	4	6	1
7	2	5	4	6	8	1	9	3
3	4	6	9	7	1	2	8	5
8	1	9	2	5	3	6	7	4
5	6	3	1	2	7	8	4	9
1	9	8	3	4	6	7	5	2
4	7	2	5	8	9	3	1	6

5	6	1	2	7	8	4	9	3
8	2	9	3	1	4	7	5	6
4	7	3	5	6	9	2	1	8
6	4	2	9	8	7	1	3	5
3	9	5	1	4	2	6	8	7
7	1	8	6	3	5	9	2	4
2	8	7	4	5	1	3	6	9
9	5	6	7	2	3	8	4	1
1	3	4	8	9	6	5	7	2

3	7	2	9	1	4	8	5	6
5	6	4	8	7	2	1	9	3
1	9	8	3	5	6	4	2	7
9	8	3	4	2	1	7	6	5
7	4	1	5	6	9	3	8	2
2	5	6	7	3	8	9	4	1
6	3	9	2	8	7	5	1	4
8	2	7	1	4	5	6	3	9
4	1	5	6	9	3	2	7	8

9	1	6	3	8	7	5	2	4
7	4	8	2	9	5	1	6	3
3	5	2	1	6	4	8	9	7
4	7	3	9	2	8	6	5	1
8	9	1	4	5	6	3	7	2
2	6	5	7	3	1	9	4	8
6	2	9	8	7	3	4	1	5
1	8	7	5	4	9	2	3	6
5	3	4	6	1	2	7	8	9

1	3	5	6	7	9	8	4	2
2	8	4	1	5	3	9	6	7
7	9	6	2	4	8	3	5	1
8	6	1	4	3	7	2	9	5
5	2	7	9	1	6	4	8	3
3	4	9	5	8	2	1	7	6
6	5	3	8	9	1	7	2	4
9	7	2	3	6	4	5	1	8
4	1	8	7	2	5	6	3	9

7	6	4	2	3	9	5	1	8
8	2	3	6	5	1	9	4	7
5	1	9	8	4	7	3	2	6
4	7	1	5	8	6	2	3	9
3	9	5	4	7	2	8	6	1
2	8	6	1	9	3	7	5	4
6	3	7	9	1	5	4	8	2
9	4	2	3	6	8	1	7	5
1	5	8	7	2	4	6	9	3

2	6	1	5	9	8	4	7	3
5	9	4	1	7	3	2	6	8
3	7	8	2	4	6	9	1	5
6	5	3	7	2	9	1	8	4
4	8	9	6	5	1	3	2	7
1	2	7	3	8	4	5	9	6
7	1	6	4	3	2	8	5	9
8	3	5	9	1	7	6	4	2
9	4	2	8	6	5	7	3	1

6	5	3	2	1	7	8	9	4
2	4	7	8	5	9	3	6	1
8	1	9	4	6	3	7	5	2
9	6	8	7	3	2	1	4	5
4	3	5	9	8	1	2	7	6
7	2	1	5	4	6	9	8	3
5	8	2	3	7	4	6	1	9
3	7	6	1	9	5	4	2	8
1	9	4	6	2	8	5	3	7

7	9	2	8	5	1	4	3	6
5	4	8	7	6	3	1	2	9
3	6	1	4	9	2	7	5	8
4	3	7	9	8	6	5	1	2
9	1	5	3	2	7	6	8	4
2	8	6	5	1	4	9	7	3
6	2	3	1	4	5	8	9	7
1	7	9	6	3	8	2	4	5
8	5	4	2	7	9	3	6	1

7	2	3	9	8	5	6	4	1
4	5	1	2	7	6	3	9	8
8	9	6	4	3	1	7	5	2
5	1	8	6	9	7	4	2	3
6	3	4	8	5	2	9	1	7
2	7	9	3	1	4	5	8	6
1	4	5	7	2	3	8	6	9
3	8	2	5	6	9	1	7	4
9	6	7	1	4	8	2	3	5

7	1	5	2	8	4	9	3	6
9	8	4	6	3	5	1	2	7
6	3	2	9	1	7	4	8	5
1	5	9	8	6	3	2	7	4
8	4	3	7	9	2	6	5	1
2	6	7	4	5	1	8	9	3
5	9	1	3	2	6	7	4	8
4	2	6	5	7	8	3	1	9
3	7	8	1	4	9	5	6	2

2	7	8	3	6	9	5	4	1
3	1	9	5	4	7	2	8	6
5	6	4	1	2	8	7	9	3
6	3	7	9	5	1	8	2	4
8	4	1	7	3	2	9	6	5
9	5	2	4	8	6	3	1	7
7	9	5	8	1	4	6	3	2
1	2	3	6	9	5	4	7	8
4	8	6	2	7	3	1	5	9

1	9	8	7	3	2	5	4	6
2	3	5	9	4	6	7	8	1
4	6	7	5	8	1	9	2	3
7	8	3	2	9	4	6	1	5
5	1	4	3	6	7	2	9	8
9	2	6	1	5	8	4	3	7
8	4	9	6	1	5	3	7	2
3	5	2	8	7	9	1	6	4
6	7	1	4	2	3	8	5	9

6	3	5	8	2	4	7	1	9
8	1	4	6	9	7	3	2	5
2	7	9	5	1	3	8	4	6
7	2	3	9	8	5	4	6	1
5	9	1	3	4	6	2	7	8
4	8	6	2	7	1	5	9	3
9	6	2	7	3	8	1	5	4
3	4	7	1	5	9	6	8	2
1	5	8	4	6	2	9	3	7

4	8	2	7	6	3	1	5	9
7	5	1	8	9	2	4	3	6
9	3	6	1	5	4	2	7	8
8	9	3	6	1	5	7	2	4
6	4	5	2	7	8	3	9	1
2	1	7	3	4	9	8	6	5
5	2	4	9	3	1	6	8	7
3	7	9	4	8	6	5	1	2
1	6	8	5	2	7	9	4	3

2	1	6	4	7	9	8	5	3
4	3	7	1	5	8	2	6	9
5	8	9	3	6	2	1	7	4
3	7	8	6	1	5	9	4	2
9	6	4	2	8	7	3	1	5
1	2	5	9	3	4	6	8	7
8	5	2	7	9	6	4	3	1
7	4	1	8	2	3	5	9	6
6	9	3	5	4	1	7	2	8

9	8	1	3	4	7	6	2	5
4	5	2	9	6	8	3	7	1
3	6	7	1	2	5	9	4	8
8	3	4	6	5	1	7	9	2
5	7	9	4	8	2	1	6	3
1	2	6	7	3	9	5	8	4
2	9	5	8	7	3	4	1	6
7	4	3	2	1	6	8	5	9
6	1	8	5	9	4	2	3	7

1	6	4	5	2	8	9	3	7
7	8	2	4	9	3	5	6	1
9	5	3	1	7	6	2	8	4
5	2	6	8	4	9	1	7	3
3	7	9	6	5	1	8	4	2
8	4	1	2	3	7	6	9	5
6	9	7	3	1	5	4	2	8
4	3	5	9	8	2	7	1	6
2	1	8	7	6	4	3	5	9

9	4	3	6	8	2	5	1	7
8	1	2	9	7	5	6	4	3
6	5	7	1	4	3	2	8	9
4	6	8	7	5	9	1	3	2
7	2	9	8	3	1	4	5	6
1	3	5	4	2	6	9	7	8
3	7	1	2	9	4	8	6	5
2	8	4	5	6	7	3	9	1
5	9	6	3	1	8	7	2	4

7	2	1	4	8	9	5	6	3
6	3	8	2	5	7	1	9	4
9	4	5	1	3	6	7	2	8
3	5	6	7	2	8	9	4	1
8	7	2	9	1	4	6	3	5
1	9	4	5	6	3	8	7	2
4	1	3	6	9	5	2	8	7
5	8	9	3	7	2	4	1	6
2	6	7	8	4	1	3	5	9

3	4	7	8	6	9	2	1	5
9	5	6	1	7	2	4	8	3
8	2	1	3	4	5	9	7	6
4	8	3	7	2	1	5	6	9
5	7	2	9	8	6	3	4	1
6	1	9	5	3	4	8	2	7
2	3	4	6	9	7	1	5	8
1	6	8	4	5	3	7	9	2
7	9	5	2	1	8	6	3	4

8	7	9	6	2	3	5	4	1
4	6	3	5	1	8	9	2	7
1	5	2	7	4	9	3	6	8
2	4	6	3	8	1	7	5	9
7	3	8	9	5	6	2	1	4
9	1	5	2	7	4	8	3	6
3	2	1	8	6	7	4	9	5
5	8	4	1	9	2	6	7	3
6	9	7	4	3	5	1	8	2

6	1	5	8	4	2	9	7	3
4	3	7	9	1	5	8	6	2
8	2	9	7	3	6	4	5	1
7	9	6	2	8	4	3	1	5
2	4	1	3	5	9	7	8	6
5	8	3	6	7	1	2	9	4
9	5	2	4	6	7	1	3	8
3	6	4	1	9	8	5	2	7
1	7	8	5	2	3	6	4	9

3	2	8	9	7	1	6	4	5
4	5	9	6	8	2	3	7	1
6	7	1	5	4	3	9	2	8
7	9	3	1	6	5	4	8	2
8	4	5	7	2	9	1	6	3
1	6	2	4	3	8	5	9	7
5	3	7	8	9	6	2	1	4
2	8	6	3	1	4	7	5	9
9	1	4	2	5	7	8	3	6

2	3	4	8	7	5	1	6	9
7	9	1	4	2	6	8	5	3
5	6	8	9	3	1	4	2	7
3	8	6	7	4	9	5	1	2
9	5	2	1	6	8	7	3	4
4	1	7	3	5	2	6	9	8
1	7	3	6	9	4	2	8	5
6	4	5	2	8	3	9	7	1
8	2	9	5	1	7	3	4	6

2	8	6	3	9	7	5	1	4
7	5	3	4	2	1	9	6	8
1	4	9	6	8	5	2	3	7
8	6	7	5	4	3	1	2	9
4	1	5	9	7	2	6	8	3
3	9	2	8	1	6	7	4	5
5	7	8	1	6	4	3	9	2
6	3	4	2	5	9	8	7	1
9	2	1	7	3	8	4	5	6

2	8	4	3	9	5	1	6	7
9	3	7	8	6	1	5	4	2
5	6	1	2	4	7	8	9	3
8	1	9	5	7	4	3	2	6
7	4	5	6	3	2	9	1	8
6	2	3	9	1	8	7	5	4
1	9	2	4	8	3	6	7	5
4	7	8	1	5	6	2	3	9
3	5	6	7	2	9	4	8	1

6	2	3	5	9	8	4	7	1
7	5	9	6	4	1	3	8	2
8	1	4	7	2	3	9	5	6
5	8	6	2	7	9	1	3	4
3	7	1	8	6	4	2	9	5
4	9	2	3	1	5	8	6	7
2	4	7	9	8	6	5	1	3
1	3	8	4	5	7	6	2	9
9	6	5	1	3	2	7	4	8

1	4	5	2	7	6	3	8	9
3	2	9	1	5	8	7	4	6
8	7	6	3	9	4	5	1	2
6	5	7	8	3	9	4	2	1
9	3	4	6	1	2	8	5	7
2	1	8	5	4	7	9	6	3
5	8	2	9	6	3	1	7	4
7	6	3	4	8	1	2	9	5
4	9	1	7	2	5	6	3	8

7	9	5	1	4	6	8	3	2
3	2	8	7	9	5	1	6	4
4	1	6	2	8	3	9	5	7
2	3	7	6	1	9	4	8	5
1	8	4	5	2	7	6	9	3
6	5	9	8	3	4	7	2	1
5	7	1	9	6	2	3	4	8
8	6	3	4	5	1	2	7	9
9	4	2	3	7	8	5	1	6

8	5	1	9	2	3	7	4	6
4	9	7	8	1	6	2	3	5
3	2	6	4	5	7	8	9	1
9	6	3	5	7	8	1	2	4
2	1	4	6	3	9	5	7	8
7	8	5	1	4	2	3	6	9
6	4	2	3	8	5	9	1	7
5	3	9	7	6	1	4	8	2
1	7	8	2	9	4	6	5	3

2	3	1	6	5	7	8	9	4
6	7	5	8	4	9	3	2	1
8	4	9	3	2	1	6	5	7
4	2	6	7	3	8	5	1	9
3	5	7	9	1	4	2	6	8
1	9	8	2	6	5	4	7	3
5	6	4	1	7	3	9	8	2
7	8	2	4	9	6	1	3	5
9	1	3	5	8	2	7	4	6

3	2	4	9	6	1	7	8	5
7	9	5	2	3	8	1	4	6
1	6	8	7	5	4	2	9	3
2	7	1	5	4	9	3	6	8
6	8	9	3	7	2	4	5	1
4	5	3	8	1	6	9	7	2
8	4	6	1	9	3	5	2	7
9	1	7	6	2	5	8	3	4
5	3	2	4	8	7	6	1	9

4	5	6	9	3	1	8	7	2
1	3	7	8	2	6	9	5	4
8	9	2	5	7	4	1	6	3
3	8	5	4	6	7	2	1	9
2	6	4	3	1	9	7	8	5
7	1	9	2	5	8	4	3	6
5	4	8	1	9	3	6	2	7
9	7	3	6	8	2	5	4	1
6	2	1	7	4	5	3	9	8

1	2	6	5	7	8	3	9	4
5	4	7	9	3	1	2	8	6
9	3	8	4	6	2	5	1	7
3	6	5	7	1	4	9	2	8
8	1	2	3	9	6	7	4	5
7	9	4	2	8	5	6	3	1
2	5	9	8	4	7	1	6	3
6	8	3	1	5	9	4	7	2
4	7	1	6	2	3	8	5	9

3	2	1	8	5	4	7	9	6
9	8	5	3	6	7	4	1	2
4	6	7	1	2	9	8	5	3
7	3	4	9	1	5	2	6	8
1	5	2	7	8	6	9	3	4
6	9	8	4	3	2	1	7	5
8	4	6	5	7	1	3	2	9
2	7	3	6	9	8	5	4	1
5	1	9	2	4	3	6	8	7

6	7	8	1	5	4	9	2	3
9	2	5	8	3	6	1	7	4
3	1	4	2	9	7	8	5	6
8	4	3	7	2	5	6	1	9
7	9	6	3	1	8	5	4	2
1	5	2	6	4	9	3	8	7
2	6	1	5	7	3	4	9	8
4	8	7	9	6	1	2	3	5
5	3	9	4	8	2	7	6	1

6	9	8	1	5	3	7	2	4
1	7	2	8	4	9	6	5	3
4	3	5	2	6	7	9	1	8
9	4	6	5	8	1	2	3	7
5	2	3	4	7	6	1	8	9
8	1	7	9	3	2	5	4	6
3	5	1	7	9	4	8	6	2
7	8	4	6	2	5	3	9	1
2	6	9	3	1	8	4	7	5

4	6	9	3	1	2	7	8	5
7	3	1	6	5	8	2	4	9
2	8	5	7	9	4	1	6	3
1	7	2	4	6	3	5	9	8
8	9	3	5	7	1	4	2	6
5	4	6	2	8	9	3	7	1
6	2	4	8	3	5	9	1	7
9	5	8	1	2	7	6	3	4
3	1	7	9	4	6	8	5	2

2	6	4	8	7	1	9	5	3
7	1	3	2	9	5	8	6	4
9	8	5	4	6	3	7	2	1
1	3	7	9	4	6	2	8	5
6	9	2	1	5	8	4	3	7
5	4	8	7	3	2	1	9	6
3	2	1	5	8	4	6	7	9
4	5	9	6	2	7	3	1	8
8	7	6	3	1	9	5	4	2

5	8	2	4	3	6	1	7	9
1	7	3	5	9	8	4	6	2
6	9	4	1	2	7	8	5	3
4	6	9	3	5	1	2	8	7
8	2	5	9	7	4	6	3	1
7	3	1	6	8	2	9	4	5
3	1	8	2	6	5	7	9	4
9	4	6	7	1	3	5	2	8
2	5	7	8	4	9	3	1	6

6	2	9	3	4	7	8	1	5
4	8	1	2	6	5	7	3	9
5	3	7	9	1	8	4	2	6
8	6	5	7	2	3	1	9	4
2	9	4	6	8	1	5	7	3
1	7	3	4	5	9	6	8	2
9	4	8	1	3	6	2	5	7
3	5	6	8	7	2	9	4	1
7	1	2	5	9	4	3	6	8

9	1	2	6	7	3	4	8	5
7	4	8	2	1	5	6	9	3
3	5	6	9	4	8	1	2	7
5	7	3	4	6	2	8	1	9
4	8	1	5	9	7	2	3	6
6	2	9	3	8	1	7	5	4
2	3	7	1	5	6	9	4	8
1	6	4	8	3	9	5	7	2
8	9	5	7	2	4	3	6	1

4	8	9	1	6	5	3	7	2
2	5	6	7	3	4	9	8	1
3	1	7	8	2	9	5	4	6
1	7	5	6	4	3	2	9	8
8	3	2	9	7	1	6	5	4
6	9	4	5	8	2	7	1	3
9	6	1	2	5	8	4	3	7
5	2	3	4	1	7	8	6	9
7	4	8	3	9	6	1	2	5

1	2	8	7	4	6	9	3	5
9	3	7	5	1	8	4	2	6
5	6	4	2	3	9	8	7	1
7	8	9	1	6	4	3	5	2
3	4	2	8	7	5	6	1	9
6	1	5	9	2	3	7	4	8
8	9	1	3	5	7	2	6	4
2	7	6	4	8	1	5	9	3
4	5	3	6	9	2	1	8	7

7	2	9	3	1	4	8	6	5
6	1	8	2	9	5	3	4	7
3	4	5	8	6	7	2	1	9
5	9	7	4	8	6	1	2	3
4	8	2	7	3	1	5	9	6
1	6	3	5	2	9	4	7	8
2	3	4	9	7	8	6	5	1
9	5	6	1	4	3	7	8	2
8	7	1	6	5	2	9	3	4

1	8	4	3	9	7	2	6	5
5	9	3	2	1	6	7	8	4
6	7	2	5	4	8	1	9	3
2	4	9	1	3	5	8	7	6
7	6	1	8	2	4	3	5	9
3	5	8	7	6	9	4	2	1
8	1	7	6	5	3	9	4	2
9	2	5	4	7	1	6	3	8
4	3	6	9	8	2	5	1	7

7	4	3	5	8	2	1	9	6
6	8	9	4	1	3	7	5	2
5	1	2	6	7	9	3	4	8
2	7	6	8	5	4	9	3	1
9	5	4	3	2	1	8	6	7
8	3	1	9	6	7	5	2	4
1	2	5	7	3	6	4	8	9
4	6	8	1	9	5	2	7	3
3	9	7	2	4	8	6	1	5

2	4	8	6	9	1	3	7	5
5	6	7	3	2	4	1	8	9
9	3	1	8	5	7	2	6	4
6	8	9	5	7	3	4	2	1
1	2	3	4	8	9	7	5	6
7	5	4	1	6	2	8	9	3
3	9	2	7	1	6	5	4	8
8	1	6	2	4	5	9	3	7
4	7	5	9	3	8	6	1	2

2	8	1	6	4	3	7	5	9
4	7	5	8	9	2	1	3	6
9	3	6	5	7	1	2	4	8
3	9	4	7	2	6	8	1	5
1	5	2	9	8	4	6	7	3
7	6	8	1	3	5	4	9	2
6	4	3	2	5	7	9	8	1
8	1	7	3	6	9	5	2	4
5	2	9	4	1	8	3	6	7

1	2	9	3	4	6	7	8	5
3	7	6	1	8	5	2	4	9
8	5	4	9	7	2	3	6	1
9	3	5	2	6	7	4	1	8
7	4	2	8	9	1	5	3	6
6	1	8	4	5	3	9	7	2
4	6	3	5	2	8	1	9	7
2	8	1	7	3	9	6	5	4
5	9	7	6	1	4	8	2	3

9	3	7	6	2	4	1	5	8
6	1	2	7	8	5	9	4	3
4	5	8	9	3	1	2	7	6
8	4	1	2	9	6	5	3	7
5	9	6	3	4	7	8	1	2
2	7	3	1	5	8	6	9	4
3	6	4	8	1	9	7	2	5
7	2	9	5	6	3	4	8	1
1	8	5	4	7	2	3	6	9

9	3	4	5	8	2	7	1	6
2	7	1	4	9	6	5	3	8
5	6	8	3	7	1	9	2	4
6	4	2	1	5	7	3	8	9
7	5	3	9	6	8	1	4	2
1	8	9	2	3	4	6	7	5
4	9	5	7	2	3	8	6	1
3	1	6	8	4	9	2	5	7
8	2	7	6	1	5	4	9	3

9	2	1	5	8	3	7	4	6
5	6	4	2	9	7	8	3	1
3	7	8	1	4	6	5	9	2
1	4	7	6	3	9	2	5	8
2	9	5	7	1	8	4	6	3
8	3	6	4	5	2	1	7	9
4	1	2	3	6	5	9	8	7
6	5	9	8	7	1	3	2	4
7	8	3	9	2	4	6	1	5

8	1	9	3	6	2	7	4	5
5	7	6	1	8	4	3	9	2
4	3	2	9	5	7	1	8	6
9	6	1	2	7	3	4	5	8
2	4	7	8	9	5	6	3	1
3	5	8	4	1	6	9	2	7
7	8	5	6	3	9	2	1	4
1	2	3	7	4	8	5	6	9
6	9	4	5	2	1	8	7	3

9	8	1	2	7	6	5	4	3
7	5	4	9	3	1	2	8	6
6	3	2	8	4	5	1	7	9
1	7	6	5	2	9	4	3	8
3	4	9	7	1	8	6	2	5
5	2	8	4	6	3	9	1	7
4	6	3	1	5	7	8	9	2
8	1	7	6	9	2	3	5	4
2	9	5	3	8	4	7	6	1

3	2	6	5	9	1	7	8	4
1	7	4	2	6	8	3	9	5
8	9	5	4	3	7	2	1	6
4	1	9	7	5	6	8	2	3
2	5	3	1	8	9	4	6	7
7	6	8	3	2	4	9	5	1
9	4	2	6	7	5	1	3	8
6	3	7	8	1	2	5	4	9
5	8	1	9	4	3	6	7	2

6	2	5	9	7	4	8	1	3
9	8	4	2	1	3	5	7	6
1	3	7	6	5	8	9	4	2
7	5	2	1	9	6	4	3	8
3	4	6	8	2	7	1	5	9
8	1	9	4	3	5	2	6	7
4	6	1	3	8	9	7	2	5
5	9	3	7	4	2	6	8	1
2	7	8	5	6	1	3	9	4

9	7	3	5	8	1	6	4	2
5	1	8	4	6	2	3	7	9
4	6	2	3	7	9	1	8	5
1	3	9	6	4	5	8	2	7
6	2	7	8	9	3	5	1	4
8	4	5	1	2	7	9	3	6
2	5	1	7	3	6	4	9	8
7	8	6	9	1	4	2	5	3
3	9	4	2	5	8	7	6	1

1	9	2	5	6	8	4	7	3
4	6	8	3	2	7	9	5	1
7	5	3	4	1	9	8	6	2
9	2	4	1	3	5	7	8	6
5	7	1	6	8	2	3	4	9
8	3	6	9	7	4	2	1	5
6	1	9	7	4	3	5	2	8
3	8	7	2	5	6	1	9	4
2	4	5	8	9	1	6	3	7

9	2	7	4	5	8	6	1	3
8	1	3	7	2	6	4	5	9
6	5	4	3	9	1	8	7	2
2	6	9	8	7	3	1	4	5
7	3	1	6	4	5	2	9	8
4	8	5	2	1	9	7	3	6
1	4	6	5	3	2	9	8	7
3	9	2	1	8	7	5	6	4
5	7	8	9	6	4	3	2	1

3	7	2	1	9	8	6	5	4
5	1	4	3	7	6	2	9	8
8	9	6	4	2	5	3	1	7
4	5	7	8	1	2	9	3	6
2	3	9	5	6	4	7	8	1
1	6	8	7	3	9	5	4	2
6	4	3	2	5	1	8	7	9
9	8	5	6	4	7	1	2	3
7	2	1	9	8	3	4	6	5

4	7	5	9	8	6	3	1	2
2	9	3	5	4	1	7	6	8
6	8	1	3	7	2	4	5	9
9	6	2	8	3	5	1	7	4
8	5	4	1	2	7	9	3	6
1	3	7	4	6	9	8	2	5
3	4	6	7	5	8	2	9	1
7	2	9	6	1	4	5	8	3
5	1	8	2	9	3	6	4	7

3	5	2	1	9	8	7	6	4
6	9	4	2	7	5	8	3	1
7	1	8	4	3	6	5	2	9
2	4	9	5	6	7	1	8	3
8	3	6	9	1	4	2	7	5
1	7	5	8	2	3	9	4	6
9	6	3	7	8	1	4	5	2
4	2	7	3	5	9	6	1	8
5	8	1	6	4	2	3	9	7

2	8	9	5	3	6	7	4	1
7	6	5	4	8	1	9	3	2
3	1	4	7	9	2	8	5	6
1	2	8	9	7	3	5	6	4
5	4	3	6	2	8	1	9	7
9	7	6	1	4	5	3	2	8
6	5	7	3	1	4	2	8	9
4	9	2	8	5	7	6	1	3
8	3	1	2	6	9	4	7	5

3	4	1	5	6	9	2	7	8
7	9	8	1	4	2	6	3	5
5	6	2	3	8	7	4	1	9
2	8	6	7	1	5	9	4	3
4	3	5	6	9	8	7	2	1
1	7	9	4	2	3	5	8	6
8	1	7	2	5	6	3	9	4
6	2	4	9	3	1	8	5	7
9	5	3	8	7	4	1	6	2

3	1	8	4	2	5	6	9	7
7	6	4	8	1	9	2	5	3
9	2	5	7	3	6	1	8	4
2	9	1	6	5	3	7	4	8
4	3	7	1	8	2	9	6	5
8	5	6	9	4	7	3	1	2
1	8	2	3	6	4	5	7	9
5	4	9	2	7	1	8	3	6
6	7	3	5	9	8	4	2	1

7	9	6	1	4	8	2	5	3
3	1	2	9	6	5	4	8	7
5	4	8	3	2	7	1	9	6
8	3	1	6	9	4	5	7	2
6	5	4	8	7	2	9	3	1
2	7	9	5	1	3	8	6	4
4	8	7	2	5	6	3	1	9
9	2	5	7	3	1	6	4	8
1	6	3	4	8	9	7	2	5

9	7	3	4	6	5	8	1	2
1	6	4	2	3	8	7	9	5
5	2	8	1	7	9	6	3	4
4	9	1	8	2	6	3	5	7
6	3	2	5	9	7	4	8	1
8	5	7	3	1	4	2	6	9
3	8	5	9	4	2	1	7	6
2	1	6	7	5	3	9	4	8
7	4	9	6	8	1	5	2	3

6	4	3	9	7	1	8	5	2
7	2	8	5	3	6	4	1	9
9	1	5	4	2	8	7	3	6
3	7	9	6	5	2	1	8	4
5	8	4	3	1	9	6	2	7
2	6	1	8	4	7	3	9	5
1	5	2	7	8	4	9	6	3
8	9	7	2	6	3	5	4	1
4	3	6	1	9	5	2	7	8

3	2	1	5	8	7	6	9	4
8	7	9	4	2	6	5	3	1
5	6	4	9	1	3	2	7	8
2	9	6	1	5	4	3	8	7
7	4	5	8	3	9	1	2	6
1	3	8	6	7	2	4	5	9
6	8	3	7	4	5	9	1	2
4	1	2	3	9	8	7	6	5
9	5	7	2	6	1	8	4	3

6	4	2	7	8	5	1	9	3
8	3	7	9	1	6	5	2	4
1	5	9	4	3	2	6	8	7
4	6	8	2	5	7	9	3	1
5	7	1	6	9	3	2	4	8
9	2	3	1	4	8	7	5	6
2	9	4	8	7	1	3	6	5
3	1	6	5	2	4	8	7	9
7	8	5	3	6	9	4	1	2

9	3	4	8	1	7	6	2	5
1	2	7	4	6	5	9	3	8
5	8	6	3	2	9	4	7	1
4	6	3	7	5	8	2	1	9
8	5	1	6	9	2	7	4	3
2	7	9	1	3	4	8	5	6
6	9	5	2	4	1	3	8	7
3	4	8	5	7	6	1	9	2
7	1	2	9	8	3	5	6	4

4	9	7	6	1	3	5	8	2
5	2	6	7	8	4	9	1	3
3	8	1	2	9	5	6	7	4
8	1	3	4	2	6	7	5	9
2	4	9	1	5	7	3	6	8
6	7	5	8	3	9	4	2	1
7	3	8	9	6	2	1	4	5
1	5	4	3	7	8	2	9	6
9	6	2	5	4	1	8	3	7

6	5	2	3	7	4	8	1	9
4	9	3	2	1	8	6	7	5
8	1	7	5	6	9	3	2	4
2	6	8	9	4	3	7	5	1
9	3	1	7	8	5	4	6	2
7	4	5	1	2	6	9	3	8
1	7	4	6	9	2	5	8	3
5	8	6	4	3	1	2	9	7
3	2	9	8	5	7	1	4	6

6	7	5	9	4	2	8	1	3
9	1	4	8	7	3	5	6	2
8	2	3	6	1	5	4	7	9
1	3	7	4	9	8	6	2	5
2	5	9	7	3	6	1	4	8
4	6	8	2	5	1	3	9	7
3	9	1	5	2	4	7	8	6
7	4	6	3	8	9	2	5	1
5	8	2	1	6	7	9	3	4

1	7	9	5	8	4	2	6	3
3	2	4	9	7	6	5	1	8
6	5	8	3	1	2	4	7	9
8	9	2	6	5	3	1	4	7
7	1	5	4	9	8	6	3	2
4	3	6	7	2	1	9	8	5
5	6	7	1	3	9	8	2	4
9	8	1	2	4	7	3	5	6
2	4	3	8	6	5	7	9	1

3	8	2	4	5	9	1	7	6
5	6	9	1	7	2	3	4	8
4	7	1	8	3	6	2	9	5
1	9	7	6	2	4	8	5	3
2	3	6	5	9	8	7	1	4
8	4	5	3	1	7	6	2	9
6	5	4	7	8	1	9	3	2
7	2	3	9	6	5	4	8	1
9	1	8	2	4	3	5	6	7

9	4	8	5	2	1	3	6	7
7	5	2	6	3	8	9	4	1
1	6	3	4	7	9	2	8	5
5	2	9	3	1	4	8	7	6
4	7	1	9	8	6	5	3	2
3	8	6	7	5	2	4	1	9
2	3	5	8	6	7	1	9	4
8	9	7	1	4	5	6	2	3
6	1	4	2	9	3	7	5	8

4	1	7	9	8	3	2	5	6
5	9	3	6	7	2	1	8	4
8	6	2	4	1	5	3	7	9
1	7	9	8	4	6	5	2	3
6	3	4	5	2	7	9	1	8
2	5	8	3	9	1	6	4	7
3	4	5	1	6	8	7	9	2
9	2	1	7	3	4	8	6	5
7	8	6	2	5	9	4	3	1

4	5	9	1	6	2	8	7	3
7	2	3	9	8	5	4	6	1
6	8	1	7	3	4	9	2	5
3	6	4	5	1	8	7	9	2
8	7	5	4	2	9	3	1	6
1	9	2	6	7	3	5	4	8
2	4	7	8	5	6	1	3	9
9	3	8	2	4	1	6	5	7
5	1	6	3	9	7	2	8	4

2	9	8	7	5	6	3	4	1
4	6	7	9	3	1	2	8	5
3	5	1	2	4	8	9	7	6
6	2	9	8	1	7	4	5	3
8	3	5	4	2	9	1	6	7
1	7	4	3	6	5	8	9	2
9	1	2	6	7	4	5	3	8
5	8	6	1	9	3	7	2	4
7	4	3	5	8	2	6	1	9

3	4	7	5	6	1	2	8	9
9	2	5	8	3	7	1	4	6
6	1	8	2	4	9	5	7	3
8	5	6	3	7	4	9	2	1
1	3	2	9	5	8	4	6	7
7	9	4	6	1	2	3	5	8
4	7	3	1	8	5	6	9	2
2	8	1	4	9	6	7	3	5
5	6	9	7	2	3	8	1	4

7	3	2	4	1	5	9	8	6
4	6	8	9	2	3	5	7	1
5	9	1	6	7	8	3	4	2
8	2	3	5	6	4	7	1	9
6	7	9	3	8	1	4	2	5
1	4	5	7	9	2	8	6	3
2	8	4	1	3	9	6	5	7
9	1	7	8	5	6	2	3	4
3	5	6	2	4	7	1	9	8

9	7	1	8	5	4	2	3	6
6	8	2	7	1	3	4	9	5
4	3	5	6	2	9	1	7	8
1	6	3	9	8	2	7	5	4
5	2	7	3	4	1	8	6	9
8	4	9	5	7	6	3	2	1
2	9	4	1	6	7	5	8	3
3	1	8	2	9	5	6	4	7
7	5	6	4	3	8	9	1	2

6	1	7	4	9	5	8	3	2
2	8	4	7	3	1	5	9	6
3	5	9	8	2	6	7	1	4
5	3	1	6	8	7	2	4	9
4	9	2	5	1	3	6	8	7
7	6	8	2	4	9	1	5	3
9	7	3	1	6	8	4	2	5
8	2	6	3	5	4	9	7	1
1	4	5	9	7	2	3	6	8

6	4	7	9	8	2	3	5	1
5	3	9	1	7	4	6	2	8
1	2	8	6	5	3	4	9	7
4	1	3	2	6	9	8	7	5
2	7	5	3	1	8	9	4	6
8	9	6	5	4	7	2	1	3
7	5	2	8	9	6	1	3	4
9	8	1	4	3	5	7	6	2
3	6	4	7	2	1	5	8	9

2	1	7	5	3	4	9	8	6
3	9	4	6	7	8	5	2	1
6	8	5	2	9	1	3	7	4
5	7	6	9	2	3	1	4	8
9	3	1	8	4	6	2	5	7
4	2	8	7	1	5	6	3	9
8	5	9	3	6	7	4	1	2
7	4	2	1	5	9	8	6	3
1	6	3	4	8	2	7	9	5

5	9	2	1	8	7	6	4	3
1	6	8	2	3	4	7	5	9
3	4	7	9	5	6	1	2	8
7	2	9	3	1	8	5	6	4
8	5	3	4	6	2	9	1	7
6	1	4	7	9	5	3	8	2
4	8	6	5	7	3	2	9	1
2	3	1	6	4	9	8	7	5
9	7	5	8	2	1	4	3	6

9	2	3	1	7	5	4	8	6
7	4	8	9	3	6	1	2	5
6	1	5	2	4	8	9	3	7
3	8	2	4	1	7	5	6	9
5	9	1	3	6	2	8	7	4
4	7	6	5	8	9	2	1	3
8	6	4	7	5	1	3	9	2
2	5	7	8	9	3	6	4	1
1	3	9	6	2	4	7	5	8

3	1	8	2	4	6	5	7	9
9	4	5	7	1	8	3	6	2
2	7	6	9	5	3	8	4	1
8	5	7	3	9	2	6	1	4
1	3	4	5	6	7	2	9	8
6	9	2	1	8	4	7	3	5
5	2	3	4	7	1	9	8	6
4	6	9	8	3	5	1	2	7
7	8	1	6	2	9	4	5	3

9	8	2	3	6	1	7	5	4
4	5	6	7	2	8	3	1	9
7	3	1	9	5	4	2	8	6
8	9	4	1	7	6	5	2	3
1	6	3	2	8	5	4	9	7
2	7	5	4	9	3	8	6	1
6	1	7	8	4	2	9	3	5
5	2	9	6	3	7	1	4	8
3	4	8	5	1	9	6	7	2

9	6	8	4	7	5	3	1	2
1	4	2	3	8	9	5	6	7
5	7	3	1	2	6	8	4	9
3	2	4	7	9	8	1	5	6
8	9	5	2	6	1	4	7	3
7	1	6	5	3	4	9	2	8
4	3	9	6	1	2	7	8	5
6	8	1	9	5	7	2	3	4
2	5	7	8	4	3	6	9	1

3	4	6	8	5	9	2	1	7
7	2	9	3	6	1	8	4	5
5	8	1	4	2	7	3	9	6
9	5	7	1	8	4	6	3	2
8	3	2	9	7	6	4	5	1
1	6	4	2	3	5	9	7	8
4	7	5	6	9	8	1	2	3
2	1	8	5	4	3	7	6	9
6	9	3	7	1	2	5	8	4

7	9	3	5	8	1	4	6	2
4	2	1	6	7	3	5	8	9
8	5	6	9	2	4	1	3	7
6	3	9	7	5	8	2	1	4
1	7	2	3	4	6	8	9	5
5	8	4	2	1	9	6	7	3
3	6	8	4	9	5	7	2	1
2	1	5	8	3	7	9	4	6
9	4	7	1	6	2	3	5	8

6	1	3	5	9	4	7	2	8
2	9	5	3	7	8	1	6	4
4	7	8	6	2	1	3	9	5
9	4	7	1	5	6	8	3	2
3	5	6	8	4	2	9	1	7
1	8	2	7	3	9	5	4	6
7	2	4	9	1	5	6	8	3
5	6	1	2	8	3	4	7	9
8	3	9	4	6	7	2	5	1

2	9	3	7	4	1	6	8	5
6	7	4	2	8	5	3	9	1
5	8	1	9	6	3	2	4	7
1	4	9	8	7	6	5	2	3
3	6	5	4	1	2	9	7	8
7	2	8	3	5	9	1	6	4
4	1	2	6	3	7	8	5	9
8	3	6	5	9	4	7	1	2
9	5	7	1	2	8	4	3	6

4	1	8	2	3	6	7	9	5
5	7	3	1	4	9	6	2	8
2	9	6	8	7	5	4	1	3
8	3	7	4	9	1	2	5	6
6	5	2	3	8	7	9	4	1
9	4	1	5	6	2	8	3	7
1	2	4	6	5	8	3	7	9
3	8	9	7	1	4	5	6	2
7	6	5	9	2	3	1	8	4

9	8	6	7	2	3	5	1	4
7	1	2	6	5	4	8	3	9
3	5	4	1	9	8	7	6	2
6	3	5	8	7	2	4	9	1
8	9	7	4	6	1	3	2	5
4	2	1	9	3	5	6	8	7
5	7	3	2	1	6	9	4	8
1	6	8	5	4	9	2	7	3
2	4	9	3	8	7	1	5	6

9	7	8	5	6	2	3	1	4
3	2	1	9	8	4	5	7	6
4	5	6	1	7	3	9	2	8
2	4	3	8	1	5	6	9	7
5	1	7	6	4	9	2	8	3
6	8	9	2	3	7	1	4	5
8	6	4	3	9	1	7	5	2
7	9	5	4	2	6	8	3	1
1	3	2	7	5	8	4	6	9

3	7	9	6	2	1	5	8	4
2	4	6	9	8	5	3	1	7
8	5	1	3	7	4	2	9	6
5	9	3	7	1	2	6	4	8
7	8	2	5	4	6	1	3	9
6	1	4	8	9	3	7	2	5
1	3	7	4	6	8	9	5	2
4	6	5	2	3	9	8	7	1
9	2	8	1	5	7	4	6	3

3	2	7	5	4	1	9	8	6
4	1	9	6	8	2	7	5	3
5	6	8	7	3	9	1	2	4
6	7	5	3	1	8	4	9	2
8	4	1	9	2	6	3	7	5
9	3	2	4	5	7	6	1	8
1	5	6	2	9	3	8	4	7
2	9	3	8	7	4	5	6	1
7	8	4	1	6	5	2	3	9

3	7	8	4	6	5	9	2	1
1	9	6	8	2	3	5	7	4
4	5	2	1	9	7	6	8	3
9	2	4	7	3	1	8	6	5
8	1	3	2	5	6	4	9	7
5	6	7	9	4	8	3	1	2
7	8	9	5	1	4	2	3	6
2	3	5	6	7	9	1	4	8
6	4	1	3	8	2	7	5	9

4	3	9	2	5	1	6	7	8
8	6	5	9	4	7	2	3	1
1	7	2	6	8	3	4	5	9
5	2	1	8	3	4	9	6	7
6	9	8	1	7	2	3	4	5
7	4	3	5	9	6	1	8	2
9	8	6	4	1	5	7	2	3
3	1	4	7	2	8	5	9	6
2	5	7	3	6	9	8	1	4

1	7	9	4	8	2	5	6	3
2	8	5	3	9	6	1	7	4
6	3	4	5	1	7	8	9	2
5	4	3	7	2	8	9	1	6
9	6	8	1	5	4	2	3	7
7	1	2	6	3	9	4	5	8
8	9	1	2	7	3	6	4	5
3	2	6	9	4	5	7	8	1
4	5	7	8	6	1	3	2	9

5	4	8	2	1	9	6	3	7
2	1	6	4	3	7	8	5	9
9	7	3	5	8	6	2	4	1
8	3	5	9	7	2	4	1	6
7	2	4	8	6	1	5	9	3
6	9	1	3	4	5	7	2	8
4	6	7	1	5	3	9	8	2
3	8	9	6	2	4	1	7	5
1	5	2	7	9	8	3	6	4

4	8	3	1	6	9	2	7	5
1	2	9	3	5	7	8	6	4
5	6	7	4	8	2	9	1	3
8	3	1	7	4	6	5	9	2
7	4	5	9	2	1	3	8	6
2	9	6	5	3	8	1	4	7
3	7	8	6	1	5	4	2	9
6	1	4	2	9	3	7	5	8
9	5	2	8	7	4	6	3	1

3	6	5	9	2	8	1	7	4
1	9	4	6	3	7	8	2	5
7	8	2	1	5	4	9	6	3
9	7	3	8	4	2	6	5	1
6	2	8	5	7	1	4	3	9
4	5	1	3	9	6	7	8	2
5	4	9	7	6	3	2	1	8
2	1	7	4	8	5	3	9	6
8	3	6	2	1	9	5	4	7

3	9	1	4	5	6	2	8	7
6	7	5	8	3	2	4	1	9
4	2	8	7	1	9	6	3	5
2	8	9	5	6	1	7	4	3
7	3	4	2	9	8	5	6	1
5	1	6	3	7	4	8	9	2
9	4	2	1	8	7	3	5	6
8	6	3	9	2	5	1	7	4
1	5	7	6	4	3	9	2	8

2	8	7	6	9	3	1	4	5
4	6	9	7	5	1	2	3	8
3	1	5	8	4	2	7	9	6
7	9	1	4	3	8	5	6	2
8	2	3	1	6	5	9	7	4
6	5	4	2	7	9	8	1	3
5	7	6	9	8	4	3	2	1
9	3	2	5	1	6	4	8	7
1	4	8	3	2	7	6	5	9

7	2	6	5	8	9	1	4	3
9	8	1	7	3	4	2	5	6
3	4	5	1	2	6	8	7	9
5	1	9	8	6	7	4	3	2
2	3	4	9	5	1	7	6	8
6	7	8	2	4	3	5	9	1
8	9	2	3	7	5	6	1	4
4	5	3	6	1	2	9	8	7
1	6	7	4	9	8	3	2	5

7	1	8	9	6	4	2	3	5
4	5	6	3	7	2	8	1	9
2	9	3	8	1	5	7	4	6
3	6	2	7	5	8	1	9	4
9	7	5	6	4	1	3	2	8
1	8	4	2	3	9	5	6	7
6	2	9	1	8	7	4	5	3
8	4	1	5	9	3	6	7	2
5	3	7	4	2	6	9	8	1

3	7	5	1	2	9	6	8	4
1	2	6	5	4	8	3	9	7
8	9	4	6	3	7	1	5	2
5	4	3	2	7	1	9	6	8
9	6	1	8	5	4	7	2	3
2	8	7	9	6	3	5	4	1
4	5	2	7	1	6	8	3	9
7	3	8	4	9	5	2	1	6
6	1	9	3	8	2	4	7	5

9	1	5	8	3	6	2	7	4
3	4	2	7	5	1	6	9	8
6	7	8	9	4	2	1	3	5
7	2	6	5	9	3	4	8	1
8	9	3	6	1	4	7	5	2
4	5	1	2	7	8	9	6	3
1	8	7	3	2	9	5	4	6
2	6	9	4	8	5	3	1	7
5	3	4	1	6	7	8	2	9

8	9	5	2	7	6	3	4	1
3	2	6	4	1	8	9	5	7
4	7	1	3	9	5	2	6	8
9	1	8	5	2	7	4	3	6
7	3	2	9	6	4	8	1	5
6	5	4	8	3	1	7	9	2
5	6	9	7	8	3	1	2	4
1	8	3	6	4	2	5	7	9
2	4	7	1	5	9	6	8	3

9	2	4	8	5	1	6	3	7
5	7	3	4	9	6	1	2	8
8	6	1	3	2	7	4	9	5
2	1	5	9	4	3	8	7	6
7	8	9	5	6	2	3	4	1
3	4	6	7	1	8	2	5	9
4	9	8	6	3	5	7	1	2
1	3	7	2	8	9	5	6	4
6	5	2	1	7	4	9	8	3

4	9	7	2	3	1	6	8	5
2	3	5	9	8	6	4	7	1
8	1	6	4	5	7	3	2	9
7	2	1	6	9	5	8	3	4
9	4	8	1	2	3	7	5	6
6	5	3	8	7	4	9	1	2
3	8	4	5	1	9	2	6	7
5	6	2	7	4	8	1	9	3
1	7	9	3	6	2	5	4	8

7	1	3	9	8	4	6	2	5
2	6	4	3	5	1	7	9	8
9	8	5	7	2	6	4	1	3
3	9	7	6	1	8	2	5	4
5	4	8	2	7	9	3	6	1
6	2	1	4	3	5	9	8	7
8	7	9	1	6	3	5	4	2
1	3	6	5	4	2	8	7	9
4	5	2	8	9	7	1	3	6

7	6	2	3	4	1	8	5	9
4	9	1	8	2	5	7	6	3
3	5	8	7	6	9	4	1	2
1	3	6	9	7	4	5	2	8
2	4	5	6	8	3	9	7	1
9	8	7	5	1	2	6	3	4
6	1	3	4	9	7	2	8	5
5	7	9	2	3	8	1	4	6
8	2	4	1	5	6	3	9	7

7	8	9	1	3	5	4	2	6
2	3	6	9	8	4	7	5	1
5	4	1	6	7	2	8	9	3
4	7	8	2	9	3	6	1	5
6	5	2	7	4	1	9	3	8
1	9	3	5	6	8	2	7	4
8	1	4	3	2	7	5	6	9
3	6	7	8	5	9	1	4	2
9	2	5	4	1	6	3	8	7

8	6	4	3	7	9	5	1	2
7	3	9	5	2	1	6	8	4
5	2	1	6	4	8	7	3	9
4	5	8	1	3	6	2	9	7
6	9	7	2	8	5	1	4	3
3	1	2	7	9	4	8	5	6
1	8	3	4	6	2	9	7	5
9	4	6	8	5	7	3	2	1
2	7	5	9	1	3	4	6	8

2	5	3	8	1	9	4	6	7
4	1	7	3	6	2	8	9	5
8	9	6	7	4	5	2	3	1
5	6	9	4	2	7	1	8	3
7	3	4	9	8	1	6	5	2
1	2	8	6	5	3	9	7	4
9	4	1	5	3	6	7	2	8
6	8	5	2	7	4	3	1	9
3	7	2	1	9	8	5	4	6

5	3	7	1	8	4	6	2	9
8	2	6	3	5	9	7	4	1
4	9	1	6	2	7	8	3	5
3	1	9	4	6	2	5	7	8
2	4	5	7	9	8	1	6	3
7	6	8	5	1	3	4	9	2
9	8	4	2	7	1	3	5	6
1	5	3	9	4	6	2	8	7
6	7	2	8	3	5	9	1	4

2	4	6	5	8	3	9	1	7
8	3	1	2	7	9	4	5	6
5	7	9	1	4	6	3	8	2
9	1	7	8	6	5	2	3	4
3	5	2	7	1	4	6	9	8
4	6	8	3	9	2	5	7	1
7	9	4	6	3	8	1	2	5
6	8	5	9	2	1	7	4	3
1	2	3	4	5	7	8	6	9

3	2	5	9	1	4	6	7	8
7	8	9	2	6	5	4	3	1
4	6	1	8	3	7	9	5	2
1	9	6	7	5	2	3	8	4
5	3	2	4	8	1	7	9	6
8	7	4	3	9	6	1	2	5
6	5	3	1	7	8	2	4	9
2	1	7	5	4	9	8	6	3
9	4	8	6	2	3	5	1	7

7	8	4	1	2	5	3	6	9
2	5	1	6	9	3	4	7	8
3	9	6	4	7	8	2	5	1
4	2	8	5	1	7	9	3	6
1	3	7	9	6	2	8	4	5
9	6	5	3	8	4	7	1	2
5	1	2	7	4	9	6	8	3
6	4	9	8	3	1	5	2	7
8	7	3	2	5	6	1	9	4

5	9	6	4	3	8	7	1	2
4	7	1	9	5	2	8	3	6
2	8	3	7	6	1	5	4	9
1	3	5	8	4	6	2	9	7
9	4	8	1	2	7	3	6	5
6	2	7	5	9	3	4	8	1
8	6	9	3	7	5	1	2	4
3	5	2	6	1	4	9	7	8
7	1	4	2	8	9	6	5	3

Printed in Great Britain
by Amazon